ZEITGESCHICHTE

Ehrenpräsidentin:
em. Univ.-Prof. Dr. Erika Weinzierl († 2014)

Herausgeber:
Univ.-Prof. DDr. Oliver Rathkolb

Redaktion:
em. Univ.-Prof. Dr. Rudolf Ardelt (Linz), ao. Univ.-Prof.[in] Mag.[a] Dr.[in] Ingrid Bauer (Salzburg/Wien), SSc Mag.[a] Dr.[in] Ingrid Böhler (Innsbruck), Dr.[in] Lucile Dreidemy (Wien), Dr.[in] Linda Erker (Wien), Prof. Dr. Michael Gehler (Hildesheim), ao. Univ.-Prof. i. R. Dr. Robert Hoffmann (Salzburg), ao. Univ.-Prof. Dr. Michael John / Koordination (Linz), Assoz. Prof.[in] Dr.[in] Birgit Kirchmayr (Linz), Dr. Oliver Kühschelm (Wien), Univ.-Prof. Dr. Ernst Langthaler (Linz), Dr.[in] Ina Markova (Wien), Univ.-Prof. Mag. Dr. Wolfgang Mueller (Wien), Univ.-Prof. Dr. Bertrand Perz (Wien), Univ.-Prof. Dr. Dieter Pohl (Klagenfurt), Univ.-Prof.[in] Dr.[in] Margit Reiter (Salzburg), Dr.[in] Lisa Rettl (Wien), Univ.-Prof. Mag. Dr. Dirk Rupnow (Innsbruck), Mag.[a] Adina Seeger (Wien), Ass.-Prof. Mag. Dr. Valentin Sima (Klagenfurt), Prof.[in] Dr.[in] Sybille Steinbacher (Frankfurt am Main), Dr. Christian H. Stifter / Rezensionsteil (Wien), Priv.-Doz.[in] Mag.[a] Dr.[in] Heidemarie Uhl (Wien), Gastprof. (FH) Priv.-Doz. Mag. Dr. Wolfgang Weber, MA, MAS (Vorarlberg), Mag. Dr. Florian Wenninger (Wien), Assoz.-Prof.[in] Mag.[a] Dr.[in] Heidrun Zettelbauer (Graz).

Peer-Review Committee (2021–2023):
Ass.-Prof.[in] Mag.[a] Dr.[in] Tina Bahovec (Institut für Geschichte, Universität Klagenfurt), Prof. Dr. Arnd Bauerkämper (Fachbereich Geschichts- und Kulturwissenschaften, Freie Universität Berlin), Günter Bischof, Ph.D. (Center Austria, University of New Orleans), Dr.[in] Regina Fritz (Institut für Zeitgeschichte, Universität Wien/Historisches Institut, Universität Bern), ao. Univ.-Prof.[in] Mag.[a] Dr.[in] Johanna Gehmacher (Institut für Zeitgeschichte, Universität Wien), Univ.-Prof. i. R. Dr. Hanns Haas (Universität Salzburg), Univ.-Prof. i. R. Dr. Ernst Hanisch (Salzburg), Univ.-Prof.[in] Mag.[a] Dr.[in] Gabriella Hauch (Institut für Geschichte, Universität Wien), Univ.-Doz. Dr. Hans Heiss (Institut für Zeitgeschichte, Universität Innsbruck), Robert G. Knight, Ph.D. (Department of Politics, History and International Relations, Loughborough University), Dr.[in] Jill Lewis (University of Wales, Swansea), Prof. Dr. Oto Luthar (Slowenische Akademie der Wissenschaften, Ljubljana), Hon.-Prof. Dr. Wolfgang Neugebauer (Dokumentationsarchiv des Österreichischen Widerstandes, Wien), Mag. Dr. Peter Pirker (Institut für Zeitgeschichte, Universität Innsbruck), Prof. Dr. Markus Reisenleitner (Department of Humanities, York University, Toronto), Dr.[in] Elisabeth Röhrlich (Institut für Geschichte, Universität Wien), ao. Univ.-Prof.[in] Dr.[in] Karin M. Schmidlechner-Lienhart (Institut für Geschichte/Zeitgeschichte, Universität Graz), Univ.-Prof. i. R. Mag. Dr. Friedrich Stadler (Wien), Prof. Dr. Gerald J. Steinacher (University of Nebraska-Lincoln), Assoz.-Prof. DDr. Werner Suppanz (Institut für Geschichte/Zeitgeschichte, Universität Graz), Univ.-Prof. Dr. Philipp Ther, MA (Institut für Osteuropäische Geschichte, Universität Wien), Prof. Dr. Stefan Troebst (Leibniz-Institut für Geschichte und Kultur des östlichen Europa, Universität Leipzig), Prof. Dr. Michael Wildt (Institut für Geschichtswissenschaften, Humboldt-Universität zu Berlin).

zeitgeschichte
49. Jg., Heft 1 (2022)

Diplomacy in Southeastern Europe Interactions during Détente

Edited by
Petra Mayrhofer and Oliver Rathkolb

V&R unipress

Vienna University Press

Contents

Petra Mayrhofer / Oliver Rathkolb
Editorial   7

Articles

Boštjan Udovič
"Going International": the (Non-)Importance of Non-Aligned Countries'
Markets in the Foreign Economic Relations of Yugoslavia 11

Tvrtko Jakovina
"Non-Alignment is not for Socialism". Yugoslav Non-Alignment during
Détente 33

Effie G. H. Pedaliu
The United States, Differentiation, and Balkan Cooperation during the
Cold War 55

Mišo Kapetanović
Yugoslav Labor Migrants Emerging as the Austrian Working Class
(1960–1980) 87

Abstracts 111

Reviews

Jan Kreisky
Dieter J. Hecht/Eleonore Lappin-Eppel/Michaela Raggam-Blesch,
Topographie der Shoah
Dieter J. Hecht/Michaela Raggam-Blesch/Heidemarie Uhl (Hg.),
Letzte Orte vor der Deportation 117

Walter Manoschek
Andrej Angrick, „Aktion 1005". Spurenbeseitigung von
NS-Massenverbrechen 1942–1945 119

Nathalie Patricia Soursos
Luciano Cheles/Alessandro Giacone (eds.), The Political Portrait.
Leadership, Image and Power 121

Authors 125

Petra Mayrhofer / Oliver Rathkolb

Editorial

In November 2020, the online symposium "European Diplomacy in Southeastern Europe. Interactions during the Détente Period (1960s–1970s)" gathered international researchers for intensive discussion of Yugoslav foreign policy in the 1960s and 1970s, with a focus on its intentions, its developments, its strategic advantages, and its limits in the context of (geo-) political, economic, and cultural circumstances during Cold War détente.

This issue of the journal *zeitgeschichte* presents current research findings based on that symposium. It offers a comprehensive survey of the role Tito's Yugoslavia played on the international level during the period. Generally, following his own road to communism after his break with Stalin in 1948, Tito sought to position Yugoslavia in between the ideological blocs.

In a recent publication on Yugoslavia's foreign relations during Cold War, historian Norman Naimark wrote that Tito even changed the character of postwar international affairs, not only by breaking up the bipolar East–West system, but also via Yugoslavia's hegemonial role in the Non-Aligned Movement (NAM).[1] Indeed, Tito led and united developing countries in Africa and Asia, positioning the NAM in the bipolar world while also benefiting Yugoslavia itself.[2] As Boštjan Udovič highlights, even economic cooperation between Yugoslavia and NAM states predominantly entailed political benefits for the Balkan state with respect to its standing on the international scene.

Moreover, Tvrtko Jakovina argues that non-alignment itself was the *leitmotiv* of all Yugoslav political goals and strategies during détente. He defines it as both a foreign policy doctrine and a constitutive element of the ideology of Tito's Yugoslavia at that time. Thus, for geostrategic reasons, both the U.S.S.R. and the United States did not underestimate the role Yugoslavia played both in the

---

1 Norman M. Naimark, "Yugoslavia in the Cold War: Afterword," in *Breaking Down Bipolarity: Yugoslavia's Foreign Relations during the Cold War,* edited by Martin Previšić (Berlin/Boston: De Gruyter Oldenbourg, 2021), 269–78, 269.
2 Robert Niebuhr, "Nonalignment as Yugoslavia's Answer to Bloc Politics," *Journal of Cold War Studies* 13 (2011) 1: 146–79.

Balkan peninsula and as a communist state outside the Soviet sphere of influence. Effie G.H. Pedaliu's contribution goes beyond Yugoslavia and analyzes the role of the Balkans in the U.S. Cold War policy of differentiation.

One example of Yugoslav non-alignment is Belgrade's active role in the Group of Neutral and Non-aligned Countries within the Helsinki process and their institutionalized non-alignment policy in Europe. Additionally, this multilateral collaboration forum eased existing tensions between Yugoslavia and neighboring Italy and Austria. Despite a cooling period in the 1970s, the flourishing development of bilateral relations between Yugoslavia and Austria after the postwar deadlock can itself be defined as an early example of détente in Europe.[3] As a side effect of this increasing bilateral cooperation but also as a result of the steady decline of the Yugoslav economy, Yugoslav labor migration to Austria became a new political issue. Perceived as a source of temporary labor, Yugoslav workers were segregated from Austrian housing facilities and social life, lacking knowledge of German. However, these *gastarbeiterji/Gastarbeiter* remained a necessary element of the Austrian economy and began to settle with their families. Whereas Yugoslavia officially declared itself a classless society, the unqualified Yugoslav workers were regarded as members of the local underclass in Austria. Mišo Kapetanović offers a fresh account of the implications of these diverging attributions of class in the relevant policy fields on the bilateral level.

---

3 Maximilian Graf and Petra Mayrhofer, "Austria and Yugoslavia in the Cold War, 1945–1991: From Postwar Cold War to Détente and Dissolution," in *Breaking Down Bipolarity: Yugoslavia's Foreign Relations during the Cold War*, edited by Martin Previšić (Berlin/Boston: De Gruyter Oldenbourg, 2021), 151–70.

Articles

Boštjan Udovič

"Going International": the (Non-)Importance of Non-Aligned Countries' Markets in the Foreign Economic Relations of Yugoslavia

I. Introduction and research problem

In recent years, the idea, issues and *differentia specifica* of the Non-Aligned Movement (hereafter NAM)[1] have gained greater interest among researchers.[2] This can be attributed to two facts: the de-ideologization of the topic and the larger access to materials in archives, political entities and other organizations relevant for studying the phenomenon of the NAM. Regarding the first thirty years after the disintegration of the bipolar system, researchers can evaluate occurrences from a larger (investigative) distance without being labeled pro/anti-communist/capitalist. The second factor is more pragmatic, since studying past phenomena is easier if you have access to the primary sources. Both factors surely

---

1 The article is a result of the research programme "Slovenia and its actors in international relations and European integrations (P5-0177)". The author thanks Jure Ramšak and two anonymous reviewers for their substantial contribution to the article. The study of materials of different official institutions does not make a clear-cut distinction between the use of the following concepts: NAM countries, developing countries, countries in development, NAM and developing countries, Third World countries, etc. What comes across from the analysis is that all these concepts are mostly used as synonyms. On the basis of the official documents, I decided to use the concept of "NAM countries" to refer to all the countries (most of which were members of the NAM) that Yugoslavia understood as (economically) developing countries and with which Yugoslavia had intensive political (and in some cases economic) relations.
2 Cf. Vladimir Unkovski-Korica, *The Economic Struggle for Power in Tito's Yugoslavia: From World War II to Non-Alignment* (London: I. B. Tauris, 2016); James Mark, Bogdan C. Iacob, Tobias Rupprecht and Ljubica Spaskovska, *1989. A Global History of Eastern Europe* (Cambridge: Cambridge University Press, 2019); Max Trecker, *Red Money for the Global South: East–South Economic Relations in the Cold War* (London: Routledge, 2020); Anna Calori, Anne-Kristin Hartmetz, Bence Kocsev, James Mark, and Jan Zofka, *Spaces of Interaction in the Globalizing Economy of the Cold War* (Oldenbourg: De Grutyer, 2019); Zvonimir Stopić, Robert Niebuhr & David Pickus, "Toward Nonalignment: The Improbable and Fateful Intersection of Yugoslavia and China in the Early Cold War, 1948–1951," *Journal of Balkan and Near Eastern Studies* 23 (2021) 2: 269–82; Jure Ramšak, "Shades of North-South Economic Détente: Non-Aligned Yugoslavia and Neutral Austria Compared" in *Socialist Yugoslavia and the Non-Aligned Movement: Social, Cultural, Political, and Economic Imaginaries*, edited by Paul Stubbs (McGill University Press, forthcoming 2022).

influence the quality of research and also provide the opportunity to evaluate past phenomena in their time and (international) political situation.

The aim of this article is to make a modest contribution to the knowledge of relations between Yugoslavia[3] and NAM countries, which were (and in some cases still are) depicted in the historiography of ex-Yugoslavia countries as a *Sonderfall* (special case).[4] Whether Yugoslavia–NAM relations were special or Yugoslavia was special in this relationship is just a question of which "ideological glasses" a researcher puts on and when (s)he analyses the events and occurrences in these relations. Whereas Tvrtko Jakovina emphasizes that Yugoslavia's role in the NAM was perceived as essential for the movement (NAM as an end in itself),[5] Jure Ramšak argues that for Yugoslavia, the NAM was more a means to "[its] prestige, [linked to the] success of global economic reform".[6]

Ramšak's statement represents the starting point of our research. Since we know that for Yugoslavia, NAM countries were a sort of political and economic laboratory, meaning that the Yugoslav leadership decided to use decolonization around the world as an opportunity to become an important political player in the global arena, I seek to answer two research questions related to Yugoslavia–NAM relations. The first (R1) deals with Yugoslavia's relationship with NAM countries and its leverage of political prestige and economic cooperation, while the second (R2) raises the question of how Yugoslavia treated NAM countries – did Yugoslavia perceive NAM countries as partners, rivals or subdued entities?

These research questions will be answered via a combination of different research methods. Firstly, a critical analysis of primary and secondary sources (Yugoslavia's foreign economic strategies, statistical data, analysis of economic flows between Yugoslavia and NAM countries, etc.) will be employed to present the basic characteristics of Yugoslav relations with the NAM. The findings obtained by the combination of these methods will be complemented by two in-depth interviews with diplomats who worked in different posts in the system of Yugoslav foreign economic relations.

The article is composed of three parts: the introduction and the presentation of the research problem is followed by a brief presentation of the Yugoslav

---

3 This term is used to avoid complication and include all of the many political reformations and renamings of the country. The name refers to the state that incorporated present-day Slovenia, Croatia, Bosnia and Herzegovina, Serbia, North Macedonia, Kosovo, and Montenegro. This (simplified) name has no bearing on the content of the article.
4 The term *Sonderfall* was coined by German politicians (West Germany) as part of the Hallstein doctrine. See more in Dušan Nećak "Jugoslavija kot 'poseben primer/Sonderfall' v zahodno-nemški zunanji politiki," *Prispevki za novejšo zgodovino* 57 (2017) 2: 111–23.
5 Tvrtko Jakovina, "LONČAR, BUDIMIR: Mr. non-aligned i jugoslavenska politika nesvrstanosti," (n. d.) <http://www.up-underground.com/wp-content/uploads/2012/06/up-underground-1920-jakovina-tvrtko-loncar-budimir.pdf> (12 June 2021).
6 Ramšak, "Shades of North-South Economic Détente", n. p.

economic particularities, forming a framework for the main part of the discussion – Yugoslav foreign economic relations with NAM countries. The article then goes on to highlight facts instrumental to understanding the economic cooperation between Yugoslavia and NAM countries and re-evaluates the propositions laid out in the introduction.

II. Prelude: a sketch of Yugoslav (economic) development(s)

Our economic analysis of Yugoslavia begins soon after the end of WWII, when political elites decided to form a country whose economic system would be a copy of the Soviet model.[7] This was also reflected in legal acts; the 1946 Constitution in article 14 established that the "means of production in the Federative People's Republic of Yugoslavia are either the property of the entire people, i.e., property in the hands of the state or the property of the people's cooperative organizations, or the property of private persons or legal entities"; article 15 emphasized that "the state directs the economic life and development of the country in accordance with a general economic plan"; while article 16 stated that "The property of the entire people is the mainstay of the state in the development of the national economy." What has to be noted is that foreign trade was no longer liberalized but directed and controlled by the state (article 14).[8]

Although it seemed that the copying of Soviet recipes worked quite well, the relations between Yugoslavia and Soviet Union began to cool off and cracked in June 1948 with the Cominform split, in which Yugoslavia was accused of straying from the path of Marxism–Leninism and taking an anti-Soviet stance.[9] Within a year, Yugoslavia was isolated – not only politically, but also economically. To avoid a serious economic crisis, the Yugoslav leadership pragmatically tuned from Eastern to Western frequencies. Western countries, especially the United States,[10] helped Yugoslavia with economic aid. In this period, Yugoslavia began to progressively change its economic structure – step by step, the command

---

7 Rudolf Bićanić, *Economic Policy in Socialist Yugoslavia* (Cambridge: Cambridge University Press, 1973).
8 "Constitution of the Federative People's Republic of Yugoslavia," n. d. <https://www.worldstatesmen.org/Yugoslavia_1946.txt> (12 June 2021).
9 Jože Pirjevec, *Jugoslavija: [1918–1992]: nastanek, razvoj ter razpad Karadjordjevićeve in Titove Jugoslavije* (Koper: Lipa, 1995); Sabrina P. Ramet, *The Three Yugoslavias: State-Building and Legitimation 1918–2005* (Washington: Woodrow Wilson Centre Press, 2006).
10 Their position if often illustrated by the phrase "Keep him afloat", attributed to British Foreign Secretary Ernest Bevin.

economy was replaced by so-called self-management,[11] sometimes also described as market socialism.[12]

Even though relations between Yugoslavia and the Soviet Union improved in 1955 and 1956 (with the Belgrade and Moscow Declarations), Yugoslavia did not reverse its economic approach to capitalist economies. Some authors claim this was because of the country's deep distrust of the Soviet Union,[13] while others argue that the structure and mentality of the Yugoslav economy was closer to Western markets,[14] since Yugoslavia was part of the capitalist world until 1939. The third explanation why Yugoslavia increasingly integrated capitalist economic instruments in its domestic economy is explained by Jože Prinčič,[15] who points out that in the 1950s, the Yugoslav economy faced strong disturbances, especially with respect to the balance of payments and debt. Attempting to overcome these imbalances, Yugoslavia adopted several progressive reforms during the 1950s, crowned by the 1961 economic reform, which enhanced the self-management system and decentralized decision-making on economic issues. All these reforms brought the Yugoslav economy closer to classical market economies.[16]

---

11 Researchers disagree on why the state decided to change decision-making regarding in its economy. While Dragutin Marsenić (Dragutin V. Marsenić, *Privredni system Jugoslavije. Peto izdanje* (Beograd: Savremena administracija, 1981), 29–32) indicates that this change happened because Yugoslavia reached a level of economic development where state control was no longer necessary, Rudolf Bićanić (Bićanić, *Economic Policy in Socialist Yugoslavia*, 63) writes that "in 1949 [there were] 217 federal and republic ministries with hundreds of directorates, running some 10,000 business organisations", suggesting that it was impossible for the state to control such a large number of enterprises. The state therefore did not renounce control voluntarily, but was forced to do so because the situation was too complex to be manageable. On the other hand, Johanna Bockman (Johanna Bockman, *Markets in the name of socialism: The Left-Wing Origins of Neoliberalism* (Stanford: Stanford University Press, 2011), 78), quoting Edvard Kardelj, argues that Yugoslavia's change in the economic system was a logical consequence of its political-economic development, since "this state of socialism [central-planning-B.U.] was just the first stage of transition and [Y]ugoslavia had begun to move to the next stage of socialism through the withering away of the state long predicted by Marxist theory." For more on this topic see also Unkovski Korica, *The Economic Struggle for Power*, 71–113).
12 Christopher Prout (Christopher Prout, *Market Socialism in Yugoslavia* (Oxford: Oxford University Press, 1985), 15 ff.) describes *market socialism* as a "balance between the social [i.e. state] control and market mechanisms".
13 Andrzej Korbonski, "COMECON," *International Conciliation* no. 549, September 1964.
14 Bićanić, *Economic Policy in Socialist Yugoslavia*.
15 Jože Prinčič, *V začaranem krogu: slovensko gospodarstvo od nove ekonomske politike do velike reforme: 1955–1970* (Ljubljana: Cankarjeva založba, 1999).
16 Vladimir Unkovski-Korica (Unkovski-Korica, "The Economic Struggle for Power", 165–67) claims that the reasons why Yugoslavia's economy remained linked to the Western/capitalist countries are to be found in internal and external variables. Firstly, there are the internal reasons: by the mid-1960s there was a large economic gap between the different parts of Yugoslavia. A symbolic break-out was the strike in Trbovlje (Slovenia) that symbolically

The decentralization of economic activities not only fragmented the economic development of Yugoslavia, but also opened a window of opportunity for those arguing for the country's "liberalization" (in economic and political terms). A wave of (political and economic) liberalization began with the new economic reform in 1965 and ended with the disbandment of the (liberal) political elites of Slovenia and Croatia in 1972. While the years after 1972 in Yugoslavia are labeled the "political frost", the economic sphere went its own way. In 1971, the Federal Assembly adopted constitutional amendments, and they became an integral part of the 1974 federal constitution and the constitutions of the constituent republics.[17] The amendments defined a new approach to economic activity with the so-called Basic Organizations of Associated Labor (BOALs), which were understood as a basic economic actor[18] and had the following characteristics: (a) they employed an average of 170 workers (meaning they were quite small entities); (b) decisions on all topics (including business activities) within BOALs were to be adopted by consensus of all workers; (c) they could merge into more complex organizations, known as OALs (Organizations of Associated Labor), or even COALs (Composite Organizations of Associated Labor).[19] Although the system was complex, it remained largely in use until the dissolution of Yugoslavia in 1991.

---

started the process of the nationalization of the Yugoslav economy. With respect to the external reasons, Unkovski-Korica explains that the Tito's winding relationship with the Soviet Union resulted from his (personal) relations with Nikita Khrushchev. When Khrushchev was replaced by Brezhnev, Tito realised that the "hard line of communism" had won and he finally decided to decouple from the politics and economics of the Soviet Union.

17 In 1976, the Associated Labor Act (Zakon o združenem delu; Official Gazette of the SFRY 53/1976) was adopted, defining the roles, activities, actions, and other aspects of BOALs, OALs and COALs. The act is colloquially known as the Little Constitution, since it implemented the provisions of the federal- and republic-level constitutions.

18 In theoretical debates, the link between an enterprise and a BOAL was presented in three different ways. The first is that an enterprise and a BOAL were the same, just the name was different, and BOALs in Yugoslavia performed the same functions as enterprises in Western/capitalist societies. The second is that an enterprise was something between a BOAL and an OAL. An enterprise merged different BOALs even if their interests differed. An enterprise was therefore a vertical integration of different BOALs. And the third is that there was no connection between an enterprise and a BOAL, since enterprises were privately owned and BOALs were owned by society, and the aim of an enterprise was profit, while the aim of a BOAL was societal development (Marsenić, *Privredni sistem Jugoslavije*, 89–91).

19 OALs linked workers of BOALs on the basis of common interests, such as the process of labor, production, business, etc. COALs merged OALs offering similar goods and services. See ibid., 80–93; Marjan Svetličič and Matija Rojec, *New forms of equity investment by Yugoslav firms in developing countries* (Ljubljana: Center za preučevanje sodelovanja z državami v razvoju, 1985).

III. Yugoslavia's foreign economic relations with NAM countries

3.1. Exposition

Rudolf Bićanić[20] classifies Yugoslav foreign economic relations into three stages: (1) state monopoly on foreign economic relations (1945–1951), (2) commercialization of foreign trade (1952–1965), and (3) integration into international division of labor (1966–1991) and defederalization of foreign trade (to the republic level), which became relevant especially after the adoption of the constitution of 1974.[21]

The first stage started in 1945 and followed the idea of a centrally planned economy. In the first six years after WWII, the government determined all of the country's foreign economic activities, which meant that the "federal government was the only seller and the only buyer in all deals between Yugoslavia and the rest of the world".[22] This approach was adopted not only because the Soviet comrades suggested it, but also because the Yugoslav government believed the devastated economy could only be revived if the state determined its development. Parallel to the idea of establishing an autarchic economy, Yugoslavia also wanted to cut the pre-war foreign trade relations (especially with Western countries) with the introduction of state monopoly.[23] This was quite important, since Yugoslavia had had an extensive trade deficit with its Western allies since the 1930s.[24]

The obstinacy of the Yugoslav leadership towards some of the Soviet claims led to a break between Yugoslavia and the Eastern bloc in 1948. The blockade had dire consequences not only for the political life of the country, but also for economic activity. In 1947, 49.1 % of Yugoslavia's total exports were to Eastern bloc countries (the Soviet Union, Czechoslovakia, Hungary, Poland, Romania, Bulgaria), and in 1948 the share amounted to 48.8 %, but in 1949 the figure dropped by two thirds, to a mere 13.8 %. A similar effect occurred with imports.[25]

---

20 Ibid., 143.
21 Although by law the federal bodies were still the only decision-makers on Yugoslavia's foreign economic relations after 1974, in practice more and more decisions on the international economic activities of BOALs, OALs and COALs were adopted on the level of the federation's six republics.
22 Ljubiša Adamović, "The Foreign Trade System of Yugoslavia," *Eastern European Economics* 20 (1982) 3–4: 147.
23 Bićanić, *Economic Policy in Socialist Yugoslavia*, 145–46.
24 Since prices within the country were administratively set and diverged from foreign prices, Yugoslavia established the so-called Equalisation Fund, which helped overcome the price differences, decreased pressures on the dinar and assisted in the smooth operation of exports and imports.
25 CIA dispatch, "Yugoslav Foreign Trade in 1949 and 1950," CIA-RDP80-00809A000700070149-8, 2011, 1–3.

In these circumstances, Yugoslavia had no other option but to turn to the West for help. Thus as early as 1949, it concluded new trade agreements with Great Britain, West Germany, France, Egypt and Israel, and renewed agreements with Sweden, Finland, Denmark, Norway, and Austria.[26] Yugoslav exports to these countries doubled in the period 1948–1949, and increased by another 10 % in the period 1949–1950.[27]

On the one hand, this (pragmatic) reorientation from the East to the West helped Yugoslavia survive economically,[28] and on the other hand it changed the mindset of the Yugoslav political elite, who realized that the classical state monopoly on foreign economic affairs was not sustainable in the long run. In 1950, Yugoslavia adopted a new economic system, easing foreign economic relations. Enterprises were still controlled by the state, but they did not receive direct instruction on which markets they should operate in, what commodities they should sell, etc.[29] This meant that after 1952, "foreign trade enterprises [...] were for the first time given opportunities to behave like real enterprises".[30]

Stalin's death in 1953 and the thawing of relations between Yugoslavia and the Eastern bloc in 1955/1956 brought a common will on both sides to improve their economic cooperation. A first step of convergence between the Soviet Union and Yugoslavia (in economic terms) was marked by the Belgrade Declaration (1955), prepared by Yugoslavia, an important aspect of which was economic relations between Yugoslavia and the Eastern bloc.[31] The declarative commitments from the Belgrade Declaration were converted to practice between 18 and 25 May 1956, when Yugoslavia participated for the first time in the session of the Council of Mutual Economic Assistance (COMECON) in East Berlin.[32] Even though Yugoslavia was only granted observer status at that session, it actively participated

---

However, this was not only a *de facto* but also a *de jure* blockade, since all members of the Eastern bloc "not only withdrew from every commercial agreement with Yugoslavia in mid-July 1949, but also refused to deliver the goods Yugoslavia had already paid for" (Ibid., 1).

26 Ibid., 3.
27 Ibid., 1–3.
28 Some of the 'invoices' were issued by the United States in the United Nations Security Council, see more in Boštjan Udovič, "'Vodili smo bitko za uresničenje našega načrta …': prispevek slovenskih stalnih predstavnikov k Organizaciji združenih narodov," *Teorija in praksa* 53 (2016) 3: 761–76.
29 Prout, *Market Socialism in Yugoslavia*, 15–17.
30 Adamović, "The Foreign Trade System of Yugoslavia", 149–50.
31 The provisions of the Moscow Declaration, adopted in Moscow on 20 July 1956, confirmed the provisions of the Belgrade Declaration. For further details, see Svetozar Rajak, "Yugoslav–Soviet Relations 1953–1957: Normalization, Comradeship, Confrontation," unpublished PhD. thesis, London School of Economics and Political Science, 2004, 181.
32 In January 1949, Yugoslavia expressed interest in COMECON membership if the Cominform Resolution of June 1948 would be rescinded. Since this did not happen, Yugoslavia did not join (Korbonski, "COMECON," 55).

in debates on coordination of plans and on the start of economic specialization. Yugoslavia also took part in the sessions of COMECON in Warsaw (18 to 22 June 1957), but it ceased to participate in COMECON activities when Soviet–Yugoslav tensions re-emerged in 1958.[33]

Figure 1: Leading forces of NAM: Indian Prime Minister Jawaharal Nehru, Tito and Egyptian President Gamal Abdel Nasser (Source: Everett Collection / picturedesk.com)

In 1958, Yugoslavia intensified its resolve to develop its own path of economic and political cooperation between the two blocs, resulting in the formation of the NAM, officially established in Belgrade in 1961. The idea originates from the conclusions of the Bandung Conference (1955), where decolonized countries in Africa and Asia met and discussed possible cooperation. Here, the idea of ties between developing countries took the podium. The outcomes of Bandung then morphed into the NAM when Yugoslavia realized that they offered a stage for a new entity in international relations – something between the East and the West. Thus the Yugoslav leadership decided to form a bloc (the most relevant partners in what would become the NAM being India, Indonesia, and Egypt) that could not only influence the development of its members but also change the global

---

33 Ibid., 16–17, 55.

(economic) structure.³⁴ During the time Yugoslavia was intensively forming the NAM system, which could serve as a platform for a new international (economic) order in its foreign trade, it conducted business as usual: on the one hand, it was increasing its foreign economic cooperation with Western countries,³⁵ and at the same time it was also increasing its economic cooperation with COMECON countries, with which it negotiated between 1962 and 1964 an asymmetric agreement that granted it associate member status, allowing it to decide on the reasons and basis for enhancing or decreasing relations with COMECON countries.³⁶

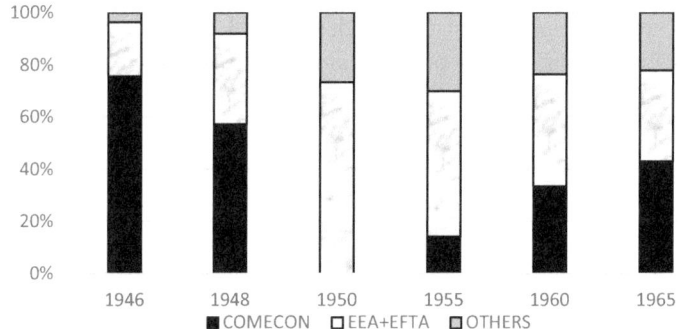

Figure 2: Structure of Yugoslav exports and imports in COMECON, EEA and EFTA and outside Europe (Source: Boštjan Udovič, based on Žarko Lazarević³⁷)

Figure 2 presents the distribution of Yugoslav exports between 1946 and 1965. The figure clearly shows that during the Cominform crisis there were no foreign economic relations with the Eastern bloc, while the share of exports to Western economies increased sharply. As soon as the situation with COMECON countries became politically normalized, Yugoslavia redirected part of its exports back to

---

34 See also Alvin Rubinstein, *Yugoslavia and the Nonaligned World* (New Jersey: Princeton University Press, 1970), 77, 313 ff.
35 See Vladimir Ivanović, "Die Beschäftigung jugoslawischer Arbeitskräfte in Österreich in den 1960er und 1970er Jahren," *zeitgeschichte* 40 (2013) 1: 35–49.
36 With respect to why Yugoslavia opted for associate membership of COMECON, Christopher Prout (Prout, *Market Socialism in Yugoslavia*, 208) explains that Yugoslav products were technologically superior to those from COMECON countries, since Yugoslavia used Western technology in its production. Achieving better quality than COMECON products, Yugoslavia had a strong export market in the Eastern bloc. However, when it comes to imports, prices in the Eastern bloc were quite high in comparison to Western countries. That is why Yugoslav "exporters preferred to sell in the East and importers to buy in the West".
37 Žarko Lazarević, "Yugoslavia: Some economic aspects of the position between East and West," *XIV International Economic History Congress, Helsinki, Finland, 21 to 25 August 2006.* <http://www.helsinki.fi/iehc2006/papers3/Lazarevic.pdf> (12 June 2021).

the East.³⁸ What is relevant for the discussion on the economic relations between Yugoslavia and NAM countries is the increasing share of NAM countries in Yugoslav exports. What is to be noted (and implicitly also confirms some of Yugoslavia's aspirations concerning NAM countries) is that whereas in 1946 Yugoslav exports and imports for all Asian and African countries accounted for just 1 %, the share increased to 14.6 % in 1961, and remained at the same level until 1965.³⁹

The 1965 economic reform also brought serious changes to foreign economic relations: (a) enterprises were allowed to freely dispose of the foreign currencies they earned; (b) enterprises and individuals could open a foreign currency account with Yugoslav banks; (c) an interbank foreign exchange market was formed; and (d) export from Yugoslavia was deregulated.⁴⁰ These changes were crowned in 1967 by the publication of the *Theses on Socio-Economic Aspects of Joint Investments by Domestic Enterprises and Production-Financial Cooperation between the Yugoslav and Foreign Economies*,⁴¹ followed by changes to different laws that allowed foreign direct investment (FDI). This was understood as an important precedent, since nobody had expected that a socialist country could/ would open its market for FDIs.⁴² Although Yugoslavia decided to only allow joint ventures in which the foreign shareholder could not have a majority stake, the decision to allow FDIs was an important step forward in the liberalization of the Yugoslav economy.⁴³

---

38 Two countries played a particularly important role in exports to the East: The Soviet Union and Czechoslovakia. In 1965, Yugoslavia and Czechoslovakia concluded an intergovernmental agreement on ferrous and non-ferrous metallurgy, which was the basis for the idea of an Adriatic oil pipeline (Jozef Sitar and Marian Sling, "Development of the Economy and Foreign Trade of the Socialist Federative Republic of Yugoslavia, 1947–1973," *Soviet and Eastern European Foreign Trade* 11 (1975) 2: 52–64).
39 Bićanić, *Economic Policy in Socialist Yugoslavia*, 172.
40 Adamović, "The Foreign Trade System of Yugoslavia," 155–159.
41 "Theses on Socio-Economic Aspects of Joint Investments by Domestic Enterprises and Production-Financial Cooperation between the Yugoslav and Foreign Economies," in *Collection of Yugoslav Law*, edited by Alexander Grličkov (Belgrade: Institute of Comparative Law, 1967), 5–10.
42 The first joint venture in Yugoslavia was concluded in 1968, see Charles R. Chittle, "Direct Foreign Investment in a Socialist Labor-Managed Economy: The Yugoslav Experience," *Weltwirtschaftliches Archiv* 111 (1975) 4: 770.
43 Charles R. Chittle (Chittle, "Direct Foreign Investment in a Socialist Labor-Managed Economy," 771–775) argues that the opening of Yugoslavia to FDIs can be attributed to the increase in industrial efficiency, knowledge and technology transfer, and employment, see also Chittle, "Direct Foreign Investment in a Socialist Labor-Managed Economy," 770–84.

3.2. Climax

In the same period, Yugoslavia tried to tie NAM countries to itself. Since these countries had their own legacies, Yugoslavia had to offer them something specific, relevant and also lucrative. The political leadership in Belgrade therefore adopted several measures to enhance economic cooperation: subsidies for NAM countries to buy Yugoslav technology, incentives to allow Yugoslav enterprises to enter NAM markets, commercial and non-commercial loans, scholarships for students from the NAM to study in Yugoslavia, etc. All these activities were performed because the Yugoslav leadership wanted to raise the prestige of Yugoslavia in NAM countries. By the end of the 1960s, the political leadership realized that politics (summit meetings, conference discussions, common declarations, etc.) would not suffice for Yugoslavia to become a leader and an important player in NAM countries. Hence they decided that Yugoslavia should cooperate with NAM countries not only politically, but also economically, thereby addressing their economic needs.

Figure 3: Delegations at the end of the first NAM conference in Belgrade, September 1961 (Source: AFP / picturedesk.com)

The shift from politics to economics in the Yugoslavia–NAM cooperation was evident at the Lusaka meeting (8 to 10 September 1970). Sponsored by Yugoslavia, the meeting promoted South–South cooperation for the first time and states adopted a Declaration on Non-Alignment and Economic Progress (NAC.CONF 3/RES14). Two years later, the provisions of the declaration were operationalized by a ministerial meeting in Georgetown (Guyana), where an Action Program for Economic Co-operation was adopted, promoting "the cultivation of spirit of self-reliance and organizing [states'] own socio-economic progress".[44] In Yugoslav-

---

44 Jure Ramšak, "Poskus drugačne globalizacije: slovensko gospodarstvo in dežele v razvoju 1970–1990," *Acta Histriae* 23 (2015) 4: 768; Laurant Zang, "The Contribution of African

NAM relations, the slogan of countries' "own socio-economic progress" was promoted by Yugoslavia, which understood this to mean independence from any of the two blocs (but dependent on Yugoslavia). What was visible from this action program was that for Yugoslavia, the NAM was no longer just a question of politics, but also a sign of economic (world) power. All these Yugoslav efforts also had an echo in the country's domestic politics.

In 1972, the International Relations Committee of the Assembly of the Socialist Republic of Slovenia held a long discussion on how Slovenia and Yugoslavia should accelerate foreign economic cooperation with NAM countries. In the documents from the committee's session of 11 November 1972, we can read:

> The cooperation between Slovenia (and Yugoslavia) and NAM countries has deteriorated in recent years. While the share of exports from Yugoslavia to NAM countries amounted to 17 % in the period 1956–1965, it decreased to 14 % of total Yugoslav exports in the next period (1966–1971). In the case of Slovenia, the figures are even worse. The total export revenue in 1966 was 324 million dinars, and in 1970 the number decreased to 312 million dinars. This is not relative but absolute deterioration. The same happened to investments and joint ventures. In 1970, Slovenia had 24 such investments, and only 9 the next year.[45]

The same document also reveals other interesting data about the cooperation between Yugoslavia and countries of the NAM, for instance:

(a) Student exchanges (Yugoslavia offered scholarships to students form NAM countries): In 1970, Yugoslavia hosted 1,250 students, 1,100 in 1971, 891 in 1972, and 836 in 1973;[46]
(b) Clearing agreements (from 1949 onwards, Yugoslavia concluded various clearing agreements with NAM countries): In 1960, there were 19 clearing agreements in place, compared to only six in 1970;
(c) Number of investments: In 1970, Yugoslavia had 1,614 different investments abroad, 378 of which were in NAM countries;[47]
(d) Number of enterprises in the NAM: Up to 1972, Yugoslavia had a total of 46 joint ventures in NAM countries (27 in Africa, nine in the Middle East, six in Latin America and four in Asia); a year later, the number decreased to 22

Diplomacy to the Non-Aligned Movement and the Group of 77," *African Journal of International Affairs* 1 (1998) 1: 1–16.
45 Ugotovitve in stališča Komisije Skupščine SRS za mednarodne odnose, št. 90-4/72, z dne 7. 11. 1972, 1–3, SI AS 1439-120, Arhiv Republike Slovenije, Ljubljana.
46 Ivo Fabinc, *Ekonomska saradnja Jugoslavije sa zemljama u razvoju 1972. i 1973. godine – ocena rezultata i osvrt na naše mogučnosti u narednom periodu (1976–1980)* (Ljubljana: Center za preučevanje sodelovanja z državami v razvoju, 1975), 50.
47 Ugotovitve in stališča Komisije Skupščine SRS za mednarodne odnose, št. 90-4/72, z dne 7. 11. 1972, 41–48, SI AS 1439-120, Arhiv Republike Slovenije, Ljubljana.

(fifteen in Africa, three in Latin America and one in the Middle East),[48] and fluctuation stopped at 31 in the period 1974–1977.[49]

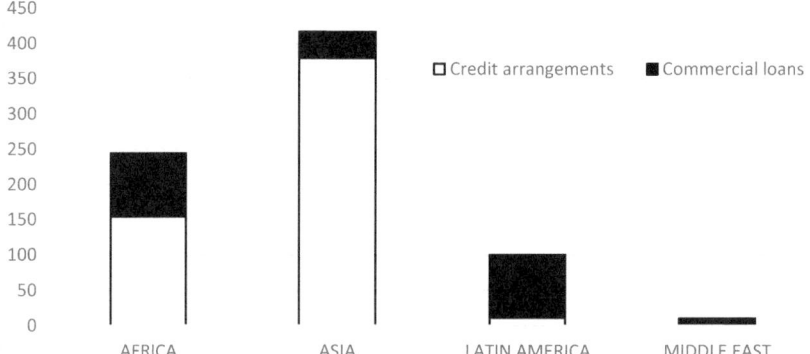

Figure 4: Structure of debt of NAM countries to Yugoslavia: commercial debts vs. credit arrangements (in USD mil.) (Source: Boštjan Udovič based on *Yugoslavia's Economic Relations with NAM Countries*[50])

In the early 1970s, not only did the intensity of economic relations between Yugoslavia and NAM countries decrease, but the Yugoslav business activities in NAM countries, frequently subsidized by Yugoslavia, were also economically ineffective.[51] This is confirmed by the findings in the 1971 document entitled *Economic Relations of Yugoslavia with NAM Countries*,[52] which reveals that from 1959 to 1970, Yugoslavia gave loans to 33 NAM countries amounting to USD 627 million, but only 40 % of the amount was repaid (for the distribution between commercial loans and credit arrangements, see Figure 4). Geographically, the main debtors

---

48 Fabinc, "Ekonomska saradnja Jugoslavije sa zemljama u razvoju 1972. i 1973," 25–26. The number of joint ventures decreased because a new law was adopted in 1973 requiring certain criteria that some of the enterprises operating in NAM countries could not meet.
49 Marjan Svetličič, *Ekonomski odnosi Jugoslavije sa zemljama u razvoju u 1976. Godini* (Ljubljana: Center za proučevanje sodelovanja z deželami v razvoju, 1977), 52. The distribution between investments in industry, trade activities and construction was almost equal (32 % of investments were in industry, 28 % in trade, 28 % in construction, and 4 % in other branches) (ibid., 54).
50 Ibid., 20.
51 An illustration of the gap between countries to which Yugoslavia exported and with which Yugoslavia had a higher form of economic cooperation is presented by Svetličič (Svetličič, "Ekonomski odnosi Jugoslavije sa zemljama u razvoju u 1976. Godini", 61), who explains that in Egypt, Iraq and Syria – which were among the top 10 export markets – Yugoslavia did not have any other (higher) form of economic cooperation (ownership or joint ventures).
52 Ekonomski odnosi Jugoslavije sa zemljama u razvoju, 17 Br. Str. Pov. 178, z dne 13. 12. 1971, SI AS 1165–881, Arhiv Republike Slovenije, Ljubljana.

were Asian countries (56 % of all loans), followed by African states (31 %), and with respect to individual countries, the main debtor was Indonesia, with 28.5 %.[53]

Since the economic reality of the cooperation between Yugoslavia and NAM countries did not meet the political expectations, the authorities went for the ideological formula. This was officially confirmed on the highest level with a statement by President Tito, who said in 1972:[54]

> When it is a question of [NAM] countries we must consider these relations for a longer period of time. We must look at the countries which are undeveloped, which have been liberated recently, as a future asset not seeking to make profits … Bearing in mind the fact that our country is industrially developing very rapidly, we must pay attention to where our *future markets* will be [emphasis added]. That is why we must invest there.

A similar statement was presented by the country's number two, Edvard Kardelj, in the case of the Slovenian enterprise Slovenijales (Slovenia-Bois) and its direct investment in Central African Republic (a country rich in high-quality wood). When the director approached Kardelj saying that Slovenijales needed state support for its operations in CAR,[55] Kardelj replied positively and highlighted that "the companies of socialist Yugoslavia don't operate in Africa like the companies from capitalist countries, with prior financial calculations of making a profit"[56] and added that "Slovenian companies should prepare their project in such a way that they contain a serious and fair attitude towards the needs of

---

53 Ibid., 4, 20.
54 Ivan Obadić, "A troubled relationship: Yugoslavia and the European Economic Community in *détente*," *European Review of History/Revue européenne d'histoire* 21 (2014) 2: 329–48.
55 Slovenijales' management requested state aid from Yugoslav authorities already one year after the creation of Slovenia-Bois (1971) – amounting to 11.6 million dinars (USD 6.6 million) for the period 1971–1973 – with an implicit threat that "unless we receive the funding, we will be forced to withdraw from the whole operation" in the CAR (Anton Petkovšek, *Poročilo o naložbah in problematiki Slovenijalesa v Centralnoafriški republiki*. Ljubljana, 7. oktober 1971, 3, SI AS 1277–48, Arhiv Republike Slovenije, Ljubljana). The pressure applied by Slovenijales paid off, and the political leadership asked Ljubljanska banka to provide the aid. The state-owned bank prepared an analysis (Niko Kavčič, *Informacija o angažiranju podjetja Slovenijales v Centralno afriški republiki*. Ljubljana, 26. oktober 1971. Arhiv Slovenije 1277–12) in the late October of 1971, revealing that the Slovenia-Bois plans for 1970 and subsequent years were unrealistic (predicting 10,000 m³ of timber for export, while only somewhere between 3,000 and 4,000 m³ were actually exported) (ibid., 2), that Slovenijales did not know the situation in the CAR, and that an exclusively export-based operation of Slovenia-Bois in the CAR would not be profitable. Furthermore, Ljubljanska banka warned that the loans to Slovenijales in 1971 accounted for 40 % of all approved consumer loans (ibid., 13). Regardless of all this, the federal authorities assisted Slovenijales in obtaining a loan, which in fact served as a subsidy for the company's operation in the CAR.
56 Edvard Kardelj, *Zapis razgovora tovariša Edvarda Kardelja s predstavniki podjetij Slovenijales […] v zvezi z njihovimi poslovnimi nastopi na afriškem trgu, zlasti v Centralni afriški republiki*. Ljubljana, 17. februar 1970, 4, SI AS 1277–12, Arhiv Republike Slovenije, Ljubljana.

developing countries for their own development".[57] Moreover, Kardelj stressed the importance of Yugoslav cooperation in the NAM, explaining that the "political conditions for our [Yugoslav-B.U.] companies in developing countries are very favorable, since these states are trying to pursue an independent foreign policy – from the East and West".[58] At the end of the conversation, Kardelj also highlighted the low absorption capacity of NAM countries, which had not managed to spend the loans received from Yugoslavia and instructed Yugoslav companies to create the conditions under which they would be able to benefit from these loans.

These political statements (followed also by others that were in line with the two presented) were quickly translated into operational documents and institutionalized practice.

In 1974, Yugoslavia adopted a new federal constitution, which became the umbrella document for the six republics, each adopting their own constitutions the same year. Article 281 of the federal Constitution (1974)[59] defined the basic framework of Yugoslavia's foreign economic relations. It may come as a surprise that this article includes (in paragraph 7) direct instructions on foreign economic relations with NAM countries, stating that the federation (through its bodies) shall "promote and stimulate cooperation *with the developing countries*, and ensure resources for the development of economic relations *with these countries and for the realisation [of] solidarity with liberation movements*" [emphasis added]. Given its inclusion in the constitution, it is clear that economic cooperation between Yugoslavia and the NAM was no longer an economic issue, but mainly one of political prestige. In subsequent years, great efforts were invested in boosting the country's economic relations with NAM countries, but with limited success.

In 1975, the Federal Secretariat for Foreign Affairs prepared three studies on the situation and challenges in economic relations between Yugoslavia and NAM countries. All three documents were evidently quite realistic with respect to the aspects hindering cooperation between Yugoslavia and NAM countries, listing the following among the most problematic issues: (a) Yugoslav enterprises' lack of interest in investing in NAM countries; (b) institutional problems and the legal framework in the host country; (c) long administrative procedures in the host country; (d) the complex system of political and economic relations between Yugoslavia and the NAM; (e) technical issues, and finally (f) a lack of information

---

57 Ibid. This was not part of the original transcript, and was added to the final version by hand.
58 Ibid., 5. See also Michael Portmann and Karlo Ruzicic – Kessler, "Yugoslavia and Its Western Neighbours 1945–1980," *zeitgeschichte* 41 (2014) 5: 296–311.
59 "Constitution of the Socialist Federal Republic of Yugoslavia," translated by Marko Pavičić, edited by Draguljob Đurovic, Ljubljana, n. d. <https://www.worldstatesmen.org/Yugoslavia-Constitution1974.pdf> (12 June 2021).

at home about the host country.⁶⁰ The latter was also exposed as one of the main problems besetting economic cooperation between Yugoslavia and NAM countries by Study No. 48124 of the Federal Secretariat for Foreign Affairs:⁶¹

> The number of permanent representations of the Yugoslav Chamber of Commerce in non-aligned and developing countries is absolutely unsatisfactory.⁶² And it is unsatisfactory because such a small number of YCC representations are not in line *with the position, nature and relevance* of Yugoslavia in non-aligned and developing countries, considering *our fundamental policy of non-alignment and our long-term economic interest* [emphasis added].

As seen from the emphasized parts of this quotation, the arguments for reinforcing economic relations between Yugoslavia and NAM countries had become politically and ideologically loaded. Under such (political) directives and pressures from the top, it was clear that the Yugoslav Chamber of Commerce would open additional offices in NAM countries in subsequent years, regardless of whether they would achieve any results or not.

In the late 1970s, Yugoslavia faced another economic crisis, which became particularly evident after Tito's death in 1980. Its GDP was stagnating, unemployment was increasing sharply, the country lacked foreign currency inflow, and its terms of trade deteriorated (see Table 1). The federal government's primary task was to stabilize the situation in Yugoslavia.⁶³ This goal was achieved, but the measures were mostly temporary, making them little more than band-aid solutions. The economic crisis also changed Yugoslavia's position on foreign economic relations, which were no longer defined primarily by political preferences, but were becoming real foreign economic relations, based on the opportunities the country had in international trade. As a consequence, the state began to actively interfere not only in the national economy but also in foreign economic relations. The political leadership adopted measures to obtain as much foreign currency as possible. This meant that although the authorities officially supported increasing foreign economic relations with NAM countries, un-

---

60 Jure Ramšak, "'Socialistična' gospodarska diplomacija: dejavnost Socialistične republike Slovenije na področju mednarodnih ekonomskih odnosov 1974–1980," *Annales – Series Historia et Sociologia* 24 (2014) 4: 733–48.
61 Savezni Sekretariat za inostrane poslove, Stanje i problemi u radu mreže naših predstavništava u inostranstvu i predlog mera za otklanjanje izvesnih nepravilnosti i negativnih pojava kao i za rešenje nekih otvorenih problema organiziranog nastupa u inostranstvu, Beograd, 18. februar 1975, 34 ff, Politička arhiva (PA) 1975, F 176, Diplomatski arhiv Ministarstva spoljnih poslova Republike Srbije (DA MSP RS), Beograd.
62 In 1974, the Yugoslav Chamber of Commerce had twenty-one representations in Western (capitalist) countries, eight in socialist countries, and sixteen in developing countries (ibid., 33).
63 Interestingly, the phrase 'economic crisis' never appeared in official discourse. Instead, the euphemism "stabilisation" was used.

officially firms were encouraged to establish contacts on a larger scale with Western, capitalist markets.

Year	GDP growth (%)	GDP p.c.**	Exports in USD mil.***	Balance of payments (% of GDP)
1978	9.04	6,276	5,671	N/A
1979	4.86	6,523	6,491	N/A
1980	2.3	6,616	8,978	-3.31
1981	1.4	6,651	10,940	-1.39
1982	0.5	6,630	10,280	-0.75
1983	-1.4	6,485	9,914	0.43
1984	1.5	6,534	10,254	0.69
1985	1.0	6,554	10,700	1.14
1986	4.1	6,780	10,353	1.39
1987	1.9	6,870	11,443	1.48
1988	-1.8	6,716	12,663	2.84
1989	-1.5	6,796	13,460	2.58
1990	-11.62	6,001	14,308	-2.69
1991*	-18.34	4,906	13,953	-1.56

*Year of the dissolution of Yugoslavia.
**Constant USD (2015) prices.
***USD at current prices.
Table 1: Economic situation in Yugoslavia in the years up to and after Tito's death (in 1980) (Source: UNCTAD database[64])

3.3. Denouement

The Westernization of the Yugoslav economy became visible to outsiders especially after 1985, when Yugoslavia proactively reoriented its foreign economic relations towards Western, capitalist countries. Data of the OECD confirm this. If exports to OECD countries accounted for 27.9 % of Yugoslavia's total exports in 1982, this share almost doubled by 1988 (52.8 %). On the other hand, this growth meant a decrease in the shares of Yugoslavia's exports to COMECON countries (from 49.9 % in 1982 to 33.1 % in 1988) and to NAM countries (from 22.1 % in 1982[65] to 14 % in 1988).[66]

However, Westernization showed not only in Yugoslav exports, but also in the number and performance indicators of Yugoslav firms abroad. According to

---

64 "UNCTAD – Statistics," <https://unctad.org/en/Pages/statistics.aspx> (13 September 2020).
65 The data about Yugoslav exports to NAM countries can be somewhat misleading, since the growth in this period is attributed to Yugoslavia's special arrangements with oil exporting countries to overcome the shortage of oil and oil products.
66 OECD, *OECD Economic Survey: Yugoslavia 1988* (Paris: OECD, 1988); OECD, *OECD Economic Survey: Yugoslavia 1990* (Paris: OECD, 1990).

Artisien et al.,[67] Yugoslavia had 287 joint ventures in Western countries in 1987 (241 in Europe, forty in North America and six in the Pacific Region), and "only" 74 companies in NAM countries (fifty-two in Africa, ten in Latin America, six in the Middle East and six in Asia). A year later (in 1988), the number of joint ventures in Western countries increased to 308, but decreased to sixty-four in NAM countries. There was also a large gap in the assets, turnover and profit/loss of Yugoslav firms abroad. In Western countries, Yugoslav companies steadily increased their assets, with total revenue more than doubling in six years (see Figure 5).

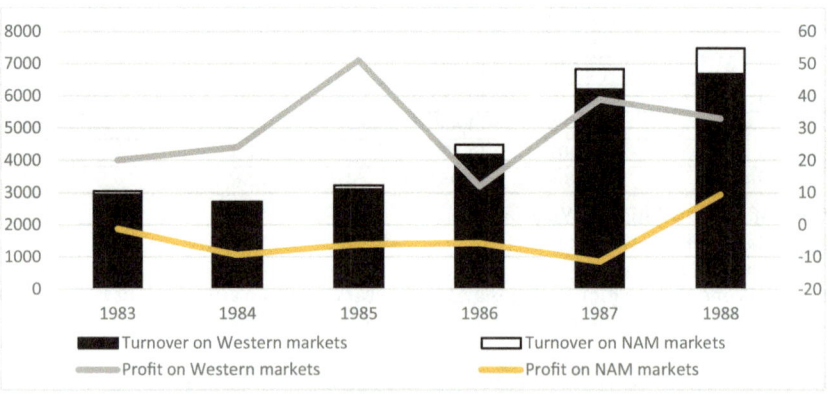

Figure 5: Total turnover and profit of Yugoslav firms abroad, 1983–1988 (in USD mil.) (Source: Artisien et al., *Yugoslav Multinationals Abroad*[68])

The second half of the 1980s revealed the fragmented and disillusioned economic and political situation in Yugoslavia. The federal authorities tried to enhance cooperation among the six constituent republics in order to re-establish the common ground that had been crumbling in practice since the very formation of Yugoslavia and disintegrated more rapidly after the adoption of the 1974 constitution. In its final years, Yugoslavia was thus only an "official structure", declaratively powerful but in fact feeble. The complexity of the system alienated the republics and individuals. As soon as the ideological glue loosened, the authority of the political elites began to vanish. This was seen in political life as well as in the economic activity of the country. With the so-called Marković reform of 1989, Yugoslavia *de jure* abandoned the policy of enhancing cooperation with NAM countries and reoriented its economy towards Western/capitalist countries.

---

67 Patrick Artisien, Carl McMillan and Matija Rojec, *Yugoslav Multinationals Abroad* (Houndmills, Basingstoke: Macmillan, 1992), 39–46.
68 Ibid., 48.

IV. Discussion and conclusions

In the introduction, we set out two research questions on the relationship between economic and political factors in Yugoslavia–NAM cooperation. The research outlined three characteristics of the cooperation between Yugoslavia and countries of the NAM:
1. The decision to enhance economic cooperation with the NAM was mainly political/ideological, and there were only few economic reasons to expand Yugoslav foreign economic relations to (economically) unknown areas. Before WWII, Yugoslav foreign economic relations were mostly focused on European countries. Between 1935 and 1939, Yugoslavia sold almost 90 % of its exports to European countries, with Germany (26.4 %) and Czechoslovakia (11.2 %) as the top two trading partners, followed by Austria (9.7 %) and Italy (9.2 %).[69] After WWII, trade was diverted towards the East for ideological reasons, neglecting Western countries. The Cominform split and the ensuing economic blockade, economic aid from Western countries, and then the thawing of relations with the Soviet Union in 1955 gradually led to the decision that Yugoslavia should no longer depend on any of the two ideological blocks and should find its own path to economic sovereignty. For this reason and because of the political ambitions of President Tito, Yugoslavia allied itself with the recently decolonized countries and formed a Third World entity that was more political than economic. But since Yugoslavia decided to assume the position of unofficial leader of the Non-Aligned Movement (together with India), it was expected that it would set an example of what economic cooperation should look like. Since this did not happen by letting things take their natural course (Yugoslav enterprises preferred Western over NAM markets), the political elite in Yugoslavia tried to solve the problem with administrative provisions, but with little success. In the words of Marko Vrhunec: "numerous developing countries with which we have good political relations are ready to offer a greater share of investment projects to Yugoslav enterprises without international calls for tender. But our private sector does not show significant interest in such businesses".[70] Today, this may sound ironic, but it illustrates quite well the situation faced by a state ideologically committed to establishing strong foreign economic cooperation with NAM countries but in practice aware that its real economic interests lay not there, but in Western markets.

---

69 CIA dispatch, "Yugoslav Foreign Trade in 1949 and 1950".
70 Informacija o nekim aktuelnim problemima u ekonomskim odnosima SFRJ sa ZUR, sa posebnim osvrtom na konkurentnost naše privrede, Savezni Sekretariat za inostranih poslova, Beograd, 23 June 1975, 3, PA 1975, F 176, DA MSP RS, Beograd.

2. The second characteristic feature of the economic cooperation between Yugoslavia and countries of the NAM was the numerous barriers to this cooperation. The first was the partially uncompetitive Yugoslav market. In the NAM, Yugoslavia was challenged by better (Western) products and foreign currency credits, higher forms of cooperation between Western economies and NAM countries, and the historical and cultural legacies NAM countries had with their former colonial rulers, now friends in business. Secondly, Yugoslav enterprises operating in NAM countries also faced problems relating to long administrative procedures in Yugoslavia and those arising from the institutional and legal environments in host (NAM) countries. Another relevant challenge was poor information about products, processes and other conditions in host countries. One such example was the case of Dawa, a Yugoslav–Kenyan joint venture[71] which in the mid-1980s was "the largest pharmaceuticals factory in Africa, contributing 5 % to Kenya's GDP and employing approximately 3 % of its workforce".[72] The problem Dawa had was that it "produced a high-quality pharmaceuticals [sic] unaware that Kenya had no registration procedure for drugs, which resulted in the influx of cheaper substitutes with resulting heavy losses".[73] This example is symptomatic of how Yugoslav bureaucracy worked. Even though Dawa was established with an agreement between the Yugoslav and Kenyan governments,[74] Yugoslav institutions did not provide enough information on how the Kenyan system worked, its challenges, pitfalls, etc.
3. The third characteristic of Yugoslavia–NAM economic cooperation was the subsidization of Yugoslav employment through investments in NAM countries. We have already outlined that Yugoslavia provided generous loans to NAM countries even though its own finances were far from solid. Most of these loans were extended, returned partially, or never returned. Diplomat and vice-president of JUBMES bank Jožef Kunič[75] argues that these loans were not intended as loans in the classical sense, but were rather a sort of

---

71 In 1975, the Slovenian enterprise Krka established its first affiliate abroad in Kenya (Dawa Kenya), Krka, "About Krka," <https://www.krka.biz/en/about-krka/company-presentation/history> (12 June 2021).
72 Artisien et al., "Yugoslav Multinationals Abroad", 43.
73 Patrick Artisien, Matija Rojec and Marjan Svetličič, "Yugoslav Foreign Direct Investment in Less Developed Countries," in *Multinational Enterprise in Less Developed Countries*, edited by Peter J. Buckley and Jeremy Clegg (Houndmills, London: MacMillan, 1991), 245–246.
74 Roberto Simonetti, Norman Clark and Watu Wamae, "Pharmaceuticals in Kenya: The Evolution of Technological Capabilities," in *Making Medicines in Africa: The Political Economy of Industrializing for Local Health*, edited by Maureen Mackintosh, Geoffrey Banda, Paola Tibandebage and Watu Wamae (London: Springer), 25–44.
75 Jožef Kunič, interviewed by Boštjan Udovič, 24 February 2017, interview in the possession of the author.

covert subsidization,[76] executed in two phases: first, Yugoslavia would give a loan to the NAM country. In the second phase, the NAM country gave deals and contracts to Yugoslav enterprises – usually paying with the Yugoslav money obtained through the loans.[77] This was a sort of win-win game. On the one hand, Yugoslavia officially received many more contracts than it would have on a competitive market, while the NAM country received new infrastructure, goods, materials, etc., paid for mostly with Yugoslav money. However, for Yugoslavia, this game had another positive outcome – artificially sustaining the level of employment, since as a socialist country it could not afford high unemployment figures.[78] This would not only put its reputation as a socialist country at stake, but would also bring pressure for political change, which the government could not allow.[79]

4. Finally, the discussion about the economic relations between Yugoslavia and NAM countries is, in my opinion, a discussion about the Hamletian difference between appearance and reality, since Yugoslavia struggled from its formation to its dissolution between its ideological postulates (as a socialist country) and its economic reality. The Kingdom of Yugoslavia's dependence on European countries prior to WWII still echoed after 1945. The attempted reorientation towards COMECON countries failed because of the Cominform, causing a lasting perception of distrust on the Yugoslav side. The establishment of the NAM was therefore an attempt to become an important player on the world stage. However, Yugoslavia understood the NAM more in (geo)political than in (geo)economic terms, whereas NAM countries also understood the NAM as an economic association. That is why Yugoslavia had to invest not only political prestige but also hard cash if it wanted to retain its position in the NAM. All in all, it could be said that for Yugoslavia the NAM

---

[76] Jožef Kunič (Ibid.) estimates that the countries only paid 15 %; the rest was covered by Yugoslavia.
[77] Kardelj, "Zapis razgovora tovariša Edvarda Kardelja s predstavniki podjetij Slovenijales."
[78] Ljubica Spaskovska, "Building a better world? Construction, labour mobility and the pursuit of collective self-reliance in the 'global South', 1950–1990," *Labor History* 59 (2018) 3: 331–51.
[79] Zvone Dragan partially disagrees with Jožef Kunič on this issue. He emphasises that Yugoslavia should be analysed in different periods, and not using a sort of cross-section analysis, since there are huge differences in the Yugoslav economy in its different stages. While confirming Kunič's observations for the 1960s and 1970s, Dragan points out that in the 1980s, when the country found itself in a very difficult economic situation, the Yugoslav government differentiated its foreign economic activities within the NAM and in developing countries into "more political" ones (i.e. with less developed non-aligned and developing countries) and "more economic" ones (i.e. with more developed non-aligned countries, especially those with oil reserves). See Zvone Dragan, interviewed by Boštjan Udovič, 14 April 2018, interview in the possession of the author; Zvone Dragan, *Od politike do diplomacije* (Ljubljana: Modrijan, 2018).

was one of the buoys that helped it float in international economic relations and, most of all, helped it sustain its political sovereignty.

To conclude, the relationship between Yugoslavia and NAM countries was a troubled one, since the two sides had different expectations going into the alliance. Yugoslavia invested in relations with NAM countries because it wanted to increase its (political) prestige in international relations, rebranding itself from a decision-taker to a decision-maker, while NAM countries decided to intensify cooperation with Yugoslavia mainly because they perceived it as a developed country able to offer donations and economic incentives. Different expectations led to a lack of common outcomes, which in the 1980s resulted in fading interest and finally a decline in these relations when Yugoslavia ceased to exist in 1991 and its members opted for Western market orientation.

Tvrtko Jakovina

"Non-Alignment is not for Socialism".
Yugoslav Non-Alignment during Détente

I.   Introduction

It took some time for Yugoslav foreign policy to become fully established in the diplomatic field after Tito and the Communist Party of Yugoslavia (CPY) came to power. The first phase was brief. Before 1948, when relations with the Soviet Union and its satellite states were severed, republican Yugoslavia was the closest and most similar to the Soviet Union of all the countries, although it was formally still pluralistic, with a parliament, a government and diplomacy that included representatives of other parties or politicians who were not members of the CPY. Although devastated, with a huge number of casualties, and undergoing the transition from a monarchy to a republic with a communist one-party government, Democratic Federal Yugoslavia (as the country was called until the end of 1945, before the new system of government was decided upon with the new Constitution, as early as 2 April 1945) expressed its desire to the Allied forces to take part in the military occupation of the "enemy territory" of the Third Reich, proposing that Austrian Carinthia, the region stretching from Yugoslavia to Italy, where there was a large "Yugoslav population", be administered by the Yugoslav Army (YA).[1] On 1 May 1945, units of the Fourth Army of the YA entered Trieste and remained in the large Italian city for forty days.[2] Istria, Rijeka, Zadar and a number of islands became part of Yugoslavia, although some time passed before the final demarcation from Italy was carried out. Thus it became evident that an ambitious and aggressive country was emerging in Southeast Europe whose war leaders were intoxicated by their own success.

After the Resolution of the Information Bureau of the Communist Parties (Cominform), the Federal People's Republic of Yugoslavia (FPRY) was initially

---

1   Nota vlade DFJ savezničkim silama o pitanju učešća Jugoslavije u vojnoj okupaciji dela austrijske teritorije, Beograd, 2. aprila 1945, *Dokumenti o spoljnoj politici SFRJ 1945* (Beograd: Jugoslavenski pregled, 1984), 23–24 [Dokumenti o spoljnoj politici].

2   Federico Tenca Montini, *Trst ne damo! Jugoslavija i Tršćansko pitanje 1945–1954* (Zagreb: Srednja Europa, 2021), 10–11.

isolated. It was mobilized, and it waited. Shocked by the fact it had lost the support of the communist world and apprehensive of its future prospects as one of Europe's poorest countries, it sought to turn its foreign policy around. The FPRY had indeed become something different, especially in the Cold War world: it was a socialist country that concluded the Balkan Pact with two NATO members in 1953, it was ready to oppose the Soviet Union, and it had reconciled with the royalist government in Greece (although it had funded and aided the anti-government guerrillas after the war). Such a country was welcomed by large parts of the world. Belgrade's revolutionary policy had not gone, but, in comparison to the recent wartime period, it was far more moderate.

The disappearance of foreign political support had made Yugoslav leaders more mature, cautious and open to cooperation with those who were different to them. Self-governing socialism, which was becoming a new ideological creed in Yugoslavia, was ostensibly what the young Marx had wanted, before Stalin's bureaucratic deviations.[3] The adapted ideological model ensured cooperation with the West and other ideological rivals, but it did not question the Yugoslav one-party system, the cult of the leader and the leading role of the Communist Party. The Soviet Union was still ideologically important to part of the population. It was still the center of the Orthodox world, regardless of the character of the new government, and it was important to everyone as the world's second superpower. A country so close to the Soviet empire certainly needed to ease and normalize relations with Moscow for economic, ideological, diplomatic, and even security reasons. The Yugoslav break with the Soviet Union and its satellites was permanent, although relations were normalized with Nikita Khrushchev in 1955 and again in the early 1960s, but this did not mean a fundamental change to the FNRY's position between the two blocs.

A position in which Yugoslavia could expect help and interest from both the West and the East and have something to offer to both was more lucrative and better suited the ambitions of its politicians. The world had redefined itself in a time when formerly great powers like France and the United Kingdom no longer even remotely carried the same weight they had until the mid-1950s. For the FPRY, the only constant was its marginal position between the East and the West, as well as its ambition. The special Yugoslav role was most visible in its leading position in the Non-Aligned Movement (NAM), founded in Belgrade in 1961, and in its activities in the United Nations. Furthermore, its special version of communism reinforced its sense of uniqueness and even importance. This was a delusion funded with and tolerated by Western aid and Moscow's and Wash-

---

3 Compare the study: Vladimir Unkovski-Korica, *The Economic Struggle for Power in Tito's Yugoslavia: From World War II to Non-alignment* (London: I.B. Tauris, 2016), chapter 2, 71–113 and further.

ington's fixation with the necessity of not permitting any territory to be lost to the opposite side in the Cold War. Such a position turned a number of small countries into more independent actors in international relations, which was something they would never have been able to become on their own. Yugoslavia was most successful in pursuing this policy, the ability to "butter its bread on both sides", with the help of the Non-Aligned Movement.

The beginnings of détente between the superpowers, and then the relaxations of strained relations on the European continent, primarily prompted by Willy Brandt's *Ostpolitik*, was actually the fulfillment of what Yugoslav diplomacy had advocated with its real leader Josip Broz Tito, who became a lifelong head of state and after the adoption of the 1974 Constitution. Relaxation, dialogue between countries with different social orders, the guarantee of existing borders, non-interference in the affairs of other countries, economic cooperation, disarmament – Belgrade adamantly promoted all this in the world through its activities within the Non-Aligned Movement. Naturally, in doing so, Yugoslavia primarily had itself within Europe in mind. This policy seemed to have become widely accepted. For the superpowers, the U.S.S.R. and the United States, non-alignment was a secondary issue, but for Yugoslavia at the beginning of the era of détente it became the main foreign policy lever, the reason why it played or could play a more important role in diplomatic relations. It was in the decade of détente that Yugoslavia managed to resolve some longstanding important issues.

Figure 1: Josip Broz Tito (Source: MARKA / Alamy Stock Photo)

In the early 1970s, with the policy of détente on the international stage, probably the most productive phase in Yugoslav diplomatic history had begun. Socialist Yugoslavia successfully used the détente policy at all levels where it was implemented: locally, in its relations with its neighbors; regionally, within the CSCE; but also as a global player, in the global policy of relaxation in which the Soviet Union and the United States played the main roles. The SFRY continued to maintain its importance as a socialist country independent of the Soviet Union. Its global influence, especially in the UN, was strengthened by its position in the Non-Aligned Movement. Both these components intertwined and influenced all three levels of diplomatic relations.

II. The beneficial impact of détente: relations with neighbors and other European countries

On 19 September 1978, Josip Broz Tito, marshal of Yugoslavia, was in the Montenegrin town of Igalo. He often went there for its health resort in the late 1970s, residing at the villa Galeb. He concluded that relations with Yugoslavia's neighbors were not particularly good. It seemed that the country was isolated between Bulgaria, Albania, Greece and Austria. "This is not favorable [...] it is very dangerous for Yugoslavia," he said.[4] Relations with Bulgaria and Albania had largely remained strained while some of the unresolved issues with other neighboring countries were settled during the détente period:

By the mid-1970s, relations with the largest neighboring country, Italy, had become completely normalized. In 1971, Tito was the first head of the Yugoslav state to visit Rome. He was also the first president of a socialist country to visit the Vatican officially. Shortly before Tito, a member of the Executive Bureau of the League of Communists (LC) Presidency, Miko Tripalo, met with representatives of political parties in Italy on 17 January 1971. All Italian parties were ready to cooperate with the LC, including the Christian Democrats. "They consider us a special communist party, different to others," Tripalo remarked. This opened up opportunities for even better cooperation between the two countries. Even then, all the participants pointed out that the border between the two countries was definite and that only technical corrections were possible. The majority of Italians "eliminated their nationalist prejudices" toward the South Slavs.[5] When Tito

---

[4] Izlaganja druga Predsednika na IV sednici Predsedništva CK SKJ, 19. septembra 1978. godine u Igalu (tekst izlaganja na osnovu magnetofonskog snimka), Josip Vrhovec's personal collection, Zagreb.

[5] Blažo Mandić, *Tito u dijalogu sa svijetom* (Novi Sad: Agencija "Mir", 2005); Izlaganje druga Mike Tripala na 71. sjednici Izvršnog biroa Predsjedništva SKJ 17. 1. 1971. godine, Brioni, Box 18, Miko Tripalo Archives, Zagreb.

arrived in Rome on 25 April 1971, soldiers were densely lined up along the Via Apia. It was a special, rarely seen honor. President Giuseppe Saragat impressed Tito with what he said, and so the latter also improvised a speech. Both Tito and the interpreter received applause. This was the beginning of the last phase in the continuous improvement in relations after 1954.[6] Tito stressed the changes in Germany, Willy Brandt's courageous policy and Germany's acceptance of the borders in Eastern Europe. Brandt was able to accept what Italians still could not, he said. Saragat replied that the border issue would be resolved during his term, which was to end that year. It took a little longer than that, but in 1975 the Treaty of Osimo de facto resolved the Yugoslav–Italian border issues. The provisional border regime ceased to exist. If we consider the period from the time the Yugoslav Army units were in Trieste and the London Agreement of 1954 to 1975, this was one of the greatest successes of Yugoslav diplomacy, even including the conquests undertaken by Yugoslav partisans during the war.[7]

Tito was also the first communist head of state to be received by Pope Paul VI, who had already received his president of the Federal Executive Council, Miko Špiljak, the first leader from a socialist country, in 1968.[8] During Tito's visit, all Yugoslav politicians were religiously rehabilitated; the excommunications in relation to the case of Archbishop Alojzije Stepinac were revoked. Tito talked with the Italians and even the pope about the Mediterranean, as it was becoming a new major area of contention in the Cold War. Here Yugoslavia was gaining in importance, not only for the Italians as one of the Mediterranean countries, but also because of the Non-Aligned Movement.

Relations with Greece, strained after the colonels' junta took power in 1967, were normalized after the regime change in 1974. Konstantinos Karamanlis believed that Soviet intervention after Tito's death was possible, and he used the prospect to improve his relations with both Turkey and Yugoslavia.[9] Greek relations with Bulgaria were better than those between Yugoslavia and its Slavic neighbor, just as the Yugoslavs and the Turks got on with each other far better

---

6 Marko Vrhunec, *Šest godina s Titom (1967–1973): Pogled s vrha i izbliza* (Zagreb–Rijeka: Nakladni zavod Globus i Adamić, 2001), 104–08; Ivan Buković Ćiro, unpublished diary, 5 April 1971; Mandić, *Tito u dijalogu*, 361; Saša Mišić, "Poseta Josipa Broza Tita Italiji 1971. godine", in *Tito – viđenja i tumačenja, zbornik radova*, edited by Olga Manojlović Pintar (Beograd: Institut za noviju istoriju Srbije i Arhiv Jugoslavije, 211), 505–20.
7 Franjo Tuđman, *Osobni dnevnik 1: 1973–1978* (Zagreb: Večernji edicija, 2001), 2 October 1975, 2 March 1977; 201; 317.
8 Hrvoje Klasić, *Mika Špiljak, revolucionar i državnik* (Zagreb: Ljevak 2019), 133–39; Vrhunec, *Šest godina s Titom*, 108–10.
9 Tvrtko Jakovina, "Neprijatelji ili samo loši susjedi? Jugoslavija i balkanske zemlje 1970-ih i 1980-ih", in *Socijalizam na klupi. Jugoslavensko društvo očima nove postjugoslavenske humanistike*, edited by Lada Duraković and Andrea Matošević (Pula–Zagreb: Srednja Europa, CKPIS, Sveučilište Jurja Dobrile u Puli, Sa(n)jam knjige u Istri, 2013), 49–50, 53–57.

than the Turks and the Greeks did. The only thing Greece and Yugoslavia had in common were problems with Albania.

Active Yugoslav participation in the preparation of the Conference on European Security and Cooperation (CSCE) and insistence on the gathering of non-aligned countries in Europe helped resolve bilateral issues with Austria, especially those pertaining to minorities. Yugoslavia was one of the most active states in the CSCE, and hence it was chosen to host the second meeting of the countries of the Helsinki Process, in Belgrade in 1977.[10]

After the severance of diplomatic relations in 1957, the German Foreign Office invoking Hallstein's doctrine, relations with the Federal Republic of Germany were politically deadened, although they continued in the field of economy. Diplomatic ties were restored in 1968. Tito visited Germany briefly in 1970, and Willy Brandt traveled to the Brijuni Islands and Belgrade in 1973, and then in 1974 a Yugoslav delegation paid a spectacularly successful visit to the new German chancellor, Helmut Schmidt, lasting several days. Relations between the two countries were good even when political ties were severed – the *Gastarbeiter* from Yugoslavia became a new link between the two countries and a source of intense contact in a positive, but also in a negative sense due to the so-called "extreme emigration". These relations strongly emphasized the connection between Bonn and Belgrade. Germany was one of the European countries that showed interest in Yugoslavia's role in the Non-Aligned Movement. The SFRY's ambassador, Budimir Lončar, was told promptly upon his arrival in Bonn in 1973 that he would be consulted regularly on world crises, immediately after the American and Soviet representatives.[11] All this made the Yugoslav issue in Germany even more interesting. Yugoslav workers were the only guest workers from a socialist country in Western Europe, and their status rapidly became regulated in the 1970s. Supplementary schools were organized, and cooperation improved.

While the ties with Germany were healthy, as long as Charles de Gaulle remained president of the French Republic, its relations with Belgrade would be strained. Yugoslavia helped the Algerians in their war for independence, and France had hitherto thought of itself as a country through which the Mediterranean Sea flowed. The Yugoslav contribution changed that image. Algeria

---

10 Radovan Vukadinović, "Beogradski sastanak konferencije o Evropskoj sigurnosti i suradnji", *Politička misao* (1979) 2: 345–60; Tvrtko Jakovina, "How Could the Non-Aligned Save Yugoslavia? The 1989 Summit of the Non-Aligned Countries in Belgrade and the Break-Up of Yugoslavia", in *European Neutrality and the Soviet Union during the Cold War*, edited by Mark Kramer et.al. (Washington DC: Lexington Books within Harvard's Cold War Studies Book Series, 2021), 195–203.

11 Tvrtko Jakovina, *Budimir Lončar: Od Preka do vrha svijeta* (Zaprešić: Fraktura, 2020), 263; 270–72; Marc Halder, *Der Titokult. Charismatische Herrschaft in sozialistischen Jugoslawien* (München: Oldenbourg Verlag, 2013), 127.

became independent in 1962 and considered its revolution to be the fifth authentic revolution of the twentieth century (along with the Soviet, the Yugoslav, the Chinese and the Cuban), partly owing to the help it received from Belgrade. The first French head of state to pay an official visit to Belgrade since the creation of the Yugoslav state was Valéry Giscard d'Estaing, in 1976, and then in 1978 Tito went on a far more spectacular first official visit to France – the first in twenty-one years.[12]

From Paris, Tito went to Portugal, a country that had become especially friendly after the overthrow of the dictatorship, just as relations with Spain were established after the death of Francisco Franco. The decade of détente was a time when relations between Yugoslavia and almost all European countries were healed and long-standing battles and misunderstandings were resolved. A completely new, favorable atmosphere in the European context was created due to the facts that Yugoslavia normalized relations with the countries with which it was at war, that these were the countries with which economic cooperation was most intense, and that border issues, including questions of war reparations, were also resolved. Even relations with Australia had been raised to a high level: in March 1973, the president of the Federal Executive Council (SIV), the Yugoslav government, Džemal Bijedić, went on a first visit to Canberra. While the Liberal Party was in power in Australia (1949–1972), Yugoslavia was treated just like any communist country, which ensured freedom for the often very extremist attitudes within immigrant circles, but this began to change with the arrival of a new administration in Australia.[13]

III. Two sides of the triangle – the United States the People's Republic of China and the relations with Yugoslavia

Relations between the SFRY and the People's Republic of China were strained practically from the time Mao Zedong came to power until the early 1970s. Then, in October 1975, Džemal Bijedić, the president of the Federal Executive Council of the SFRY, traveled to Beijing, where he had a long conversation with President Mao.[14] Hua Guofeng's rise to power in Beijing meant a complete change in relations with the SFRY. Tito was the first statesman to visit the still unfinished mausoleum of Mao Zedong in Tiananmen Square in 1977. Tito's waiter Gojko

---

12 Mandić, *Tito u dijalogu*, 556–63.
13 Nikola Mate Tokić, *Croatian Radical Separatism and Diaspora Terrorism During the Cold War* (West Lafayette: Purdue University, 2020), 148–50; Husnija Kamberović, *Džemal Bijedić: politička biografija* (Mostar: Muzej Hercegovine Mostar, 2012), 318–20.
14 Ibid., 348–50.

Karna said that on the Great Wall of China he asked him to open Ružica, his favorite Brijuni wine. "Who would have thought only a few years ago that I would be here, drinking Ružica," the Yugoslav marshal said with satisfaction during a very important meeting that Yugoslavia saw as an ideological victory.[15] Hua Guofeng's eight-day visit to Yugoslavia followed on 21 August 1978. The welcome in Belgrade was warm, but not spectacular. However, the next day, around half a million people were dragged to the streets to ensure a spectacle. Thirty folklore societies performed their dances. Hua praised Tito as the leader of the Non-Aligned Movement.[16] He visited several parts of the country and gave a speech in Macedonia. The Albanians then accused Hua Guofeng of having delivered his speech in Macedonia for the sole purpose of provoking Enver Hoxha, with whom the Chinese had severed all ties. It had little effect on the world communist movement, but it further isolated Tirana, which from that moment on represented only a small strategic danger to Yugoslav security. During a visit to Zagreb and the large Rade Končar factory, the director and later the last president of the Federal Executive Council, the Yugoslav government, Ante Marković, believing that his company might impress the Chinese, said he felt that "the Chinese market was opening up."[17] TASS reacted strongly to all this. "The Chinese and the Balkan powder keg" screamed the headlines in response to the creation of an anti-Soviet alliance.[18] During Brezhnev's visit to Sofia, the Yugoslav attitude toward the armed conflict between China and Vietnam in 1979 was described by Bulgaria and the Soviet Union as "bourgeois-nationalist and non-class," clearly demonstrating how deep the divisions between Belgrade and Moscow were over doctrinal issues, how important China was becoming, and how quickly Yugoslavia became involved in the conflict, which it had done before, not always to its own benefit.[19]

Relations with the United States had been relatively clearly defined since 1948. There had been ups and downs, but it was quite clear that an independent Yugoslavia and the Adriatic were under the control of the Yugoslav National Army (JNA) and not the Warsaw Pact, a situation favorable to the United States. A country developing its own interpretation of Marxism was not a concern for the policies of the Western world. In one of the countless American analyses on

---

15 Gojko Karna, interviewed by Tvrtko Jakovina, 90 minutes, 6 November 2020, interview in the possession of the author.
16 Buković Ćiro, diary, 22 August 1978.
17 Tvrtko Jakovina, *Treća strana Hladnog rata* (Zaprešić: Fraktura, 2013), 649–50.
18 Tuđman, "*Osobni dnevnik 1,*" 29 August 1978, 404; Mandić, *Tito u dijalogu*, 533–50; Blažo Mandić, *S Titom: Četvrt veka u Kabinetu* (Beograd: Dan Graf, 2012), 96–98.
19 Pregled obaveštajnih elemenata za procenu bezbednosnog položaja SFRJ, Služba za istraživanje i dokumentaciju, SSIP, Str. pov., br. 843, 29 December 1979, Josip Vrhovac's personal collection, Zagreb.

the possible development of the situation in Yugoslavia once Tito was gone, it was estimated that the country's survival was necessary to suppress Soviet expansion into an area that Moscow still considered strategically important or a territory to which it was entitled. The destabilization of the SFRY was to help Moscow in that it could activate forces that would call on the Soviets for brotherly intervention. The change in the position of the SFRY, as was analyzed in 1972, would be "the first significant shift in the postwar European power balance," which could increase the cohesion of NATO but also force individual member countries to seek direct agreement with Moscow.[20] At a time when a sharp conflict between old and new cadres, between the reformists and the proponents of a centralized state, was raging in the country, the West's assessment of the situation in Yugoslavia boiled down to the fact that support for federal institutions needed to be secured, avoiding at all costs the sense that the Slovenian or Croatian concept of a more liberal, open development would be in U.S. interests. The fall of the rule of the LC and the Communists in general could provoke Soviet intervention, and that was not in the interests of the West. The existing government was a guarantor of cohesion on the domestic level and it was active in combating nationalism. Perhaps the most important thing was the conclusion and the recommendation that non-alignment should be strengthened and encouraged "while gradually and in a controlled manner proliferating and strengthening ties with Western Europe and the United States." For Washington, only non-alignment that was not aimed at strengthening the East would be acceptable. However, it was clear where American priorities lay and how various Yugoslav policies were recognized as useful or usable for the West. Although relations were not always idyllic – Tito openly criticized U.S. Ambassador Silberman, who was replaced by Lawrence S. Eagleburger after a little over a year spent in office (May 1975 – December 1976) – there were no strategic disruptions in U.S.-Yugoslav relations.[21]

The 1970s and the period of détente were a time of extremely frequent meetings on the highest level. During President Jimmy Carter's time in office, this was more evident than ever before. In July 1978, Carter told Yugoslav parliamentarians that "Yugoslavia's security was of world interest" and spoke of Tito as a friend, as Franjo Tuđman, who always had a positive attitude toward Tito, wrote in his diary.[22] Tito visited America in 1971 and 1978, while U.S. President Nixon visited Yugoslavia in 1970, Gerald Ford in 1975, and Carter in 1980. Others traveled too, and hence the concentration of visits on the highest level was

---

20 A. Ross Johnson and Arnold L. Horelick, *Communist Political Succession: A Report prepared for the Department of State* (Santa Monica: RAND Report R-1958-DOS, June 1972).
21 Ivo Visković, "1970s and 1980s as the Peak in Serbian-American Relations", in *125 Years of Diplomatic Relations Between the USA and Serbia*, edited by Ljubinka Trgovčević (Beograd: Faculty of Political Sciences, University of Belgrade, 2008), 143–46.
22 Tuđman, "*Osobni dnevnik 1*," 19 July 1978, 402.

comparable only to those between Yugoslavia and the U.S.S.R. David Rockefeller visited in 1973, Henry Kissinger and Senator Edward Kennedy in 1974, SIV President Džemal Bijedić went on an official visit to the United States in 1975, where he met with President Ford, and U.S. Secretary of the Treasury William Simon traveled to Belgrade in June 1975. In 1977, Vice President Walter Mondale made a visit to Belgrade, followed by another by Secretary of Defense Harold Brown. In 1976, the Americans sold fifteen TOW anti-tank missile systems to the SFRY, each with ten charges and costing $100,000. The weapon was new, an indicator that the United States was not giving up on its alliance with Yugoslavia.[23] There were also numerous sideline meetings at large conferences. Both sides obviously wanted to provide reminders of how important they were to the other party.[24]

During the last months of Tito's life, which coincided with the end of the détente period, the Yugoslav government once again realized how sensitive their position was. The declaration on the Soviet entry into Afghanistan in 1979 was probably the last political act of the marshal of Yugoslavia. Afghanistan was socialist, it was not a part of the blocs, it was non-aligned, and the U.S.S.R. still intervened. The American media very often noted the similarity between Afghanistan and Yugoslavia. The détente thus meant the deepening and establishing of good relations, the recognition of what the SFRY was. The only superpower which was not happy with such a successful policy was Moscow.

IV. Fear of the Soviet Union

Yugoslavia often held meetings on the highest level with the Soviet Union in the 1970s, even more so than with the United States. The president of the SIV, Mitja Ribičič, visited the U.S.S.R. in 1971, as did Mirko Tepavac, the state secretary for foreign affairs between 23 and 27 February 1971. Leonid Brezhnev visited Yugoslavia on 25 September 1971, at a time when an internal crisis, the reform movement in Croatia, later called the Croatian Spring, was threatening to destabilize the SFRY.[25] At the time, intelligence speculation pointed out that the

---

23 Buković Ćiro, diary, 17 May 1976.
24 Mandić, *Tito u dijalogu*, 584–99; Kamberović, *Džemal Bijedić*, 346–47; Jakovina, *Budimir Lončar*, 336–38; 347–48. *Hronika međunarodnih događaja 1973–1978* (Beograd: Institut za međunarodnu politiku i privredu).
25 There are many publications on the reform movement in SR Croatia (the Croatian Spring) in the early 1970s. For the foreign policy aspect of it see Tvrtko Jakovina (ed.), *Hrvatsko proljeće – četrdeset godina poslije* (Zagreb: Centar za demokraciju i pravo "Miko Tripalo", Filozofski fakultet, Pravni fakultet, Fakultet političkih znanosti, 2012); Ante Batović, *The Croatian Spring, Nationalism, Repression and Foreign Policy under Tito* (London: I.B. Tauris, 2017).

Soviet Union had made a mistake when it focused exclusively on the eastern parts of Yugoslavia, because the western republics Croatia and Slovenia might have been willing to cooperate in breaking up Yugoslavia in exchange for their independence. The Soviet Union became increasingly interested in the western part of the country precisely because of the Mediterranean. Such speculations, which provoked debate among the Yugoslav leadership, were supported by the proclamation of the right-wing pro-fascist Croat emigration, whose leader Ivan Jelić stated in West Berlin that the twenty-five-year wait for the West to help Croats was obviously futile in the light of the excellent cooperation with Tito (who was, however, also a Croat), and hence cooperation with the Soviet Union, if that was the way to achieve the goal of the creation of a Croatian state, would be far more opportune.[26] Soviet politics, far more directly than any other, interfered in internal relations, made speculations, and made Belgrade nervous.

What remained hidden from the public during the détente period was strong pressures and hostile secret communication. Tito returned the visit to Moscow as early as July 1972.[27] What was published publicly in press releases was fairly standard. State Secretary for Foreign Affairs Mirko Tepavac and Andrei Gromyko praised the Finns, who organized the meeting and multilateral consultations on a "pan-European conference," and criticized Israel for not respecting UN declarations. Tito and Brezhnev also pointed out the efforts for lasting peace and security in the Balkans and for the nuclear demilitarization of the peninsula and emphasized that they were against the American intervention in Indochina, for strengthening the role of the UN, for the admission of the People's Republic of China to the World Organization, for the admission of North Korea, and for the simultaneous admission of East and West Germany to the UN. They praised the Ostpolitik and the negotiations of European countries. Everything seemed normal, indeed even more than normal.[28] The only embarrassing thing was Brezhnev's attempt to use his seven points as a platform for talks, instead of the previous agreements, which had always been invoked in mutual statements since 1955 and 1956. For the SFRY, the Belgrade and the Moscow declarations were the starting point, a guarantee of its independent position. According to the head of Tito's cabinet, Brezhnev underlined that the SFRY "as a non-aligned country means a lot in the world," which was certainly something they wanted to hear in

---

26 Tokić, *Croatian Radical Separatism*, 121–23.
27 Veljko Mićunović, *Moskovske godine 1969/1971* (Beograd: Jugoslovenska revija, 1984), 142–45; Tvrtko Jakovina, "Jugoslavija, Hrvatsko proljeće i Sovjeti u detantu", *Kolo* 4 (zima 2005): 173–80.
28 Kominike o poseti Državnog sekretara za inostrane poslove SFRJ Sovjetskom Savezu, SSIP, 27 February 1971; Jugoslovensko-sovjetska izjava, 25 September 1971, Budimir Lončar's personal collection, Zagreb.

Belgrade.[29] At the same time, SFRY Ambassador to Moscow Veljko Mićunović reported that the Soviet Union referred to self-governing socialism as "market socialism," that when one took into consideration the unemployment, the strikes, the emigration of labor to the West, the national conflicts, and even the freedom of the press, countless Western films and books, the Yugoslav system was unstable, problematic, and non-socialist. Yugoslavia was not even included in their analyses of socialist societies. It was an approach different to the traditional, continuous attack on revisionist or anti-internationalist practices.[30]

A top-level meeting (about which high-ranking politicians in Zagreb were informed on 22 June 1971) further aggravated the problematic nature of Yugoslav–Soviet relations at a critical time for the SFRY. As Ivan Buković, then director of the Chamber of Commerce and a member of the highest party bodies of the Socialist Republic of Croatia, put it, both great powers were interested in a split in Yugoslavia, except that the Americans were also fine with "Yugoslavia as it was, holding the Adriatic", although they would have preferred a change in the political system. The Soviets, on the other hand, needed the Adriatic, "they think they have a right to it as a socialist territory." "They are putting pressure on us because of the Adriatic," they wanted influence over the army, preferably without applying military force. Yugoslav self-governing socialism continued to be a destabilizing factor ideologically; self-government was "denigrated" by the Soviets, who considered it disastrous in "military-strategic" terms. "Because of that, the Soviet intelligence service is working more aggressively and nervously"; it was the most active it had been since 1940, reported the head of the military intelligence service, General Ivan Mišković, and the federal secretary of national defense, General Nikola Ljubičić.[31] A military exercise was held in 1971 with the countries of the Eastern Bloc, with a large concentration of planes and tanks near the Yugoslav border, under the working title of "Brotherly Aid to Yugoslavia." At that time, the Soviet Union perceived all the reform processes, any changes that had begun, the succession of generations, as a matter concerning Moscow. The Czechoslovak military delegations withdrew from the visits they had already agreed on, and the media in the East dramatized the situation in Yugoslavia. Tito, on the other hand, demanded that those who were responsible and connected to the Soviet Union in any inappropriate way be removed from office "one step at a time."

Of all the big countries, the Soviet Union most openly denied and belittled the policy of non-alignment, and continuously challenged Yugoslavia with a fab-

---

29 Vrhunec, *Šest godina s Titom*, 116.
30 Mićunović, *Moskovske godine*, 80.
31 Izvještaj političkog aktiva, in Buković Ćiro, diary, 22 June 1971.

ricated dilemma to decide whether it was a socialist or a non-aligned country.[32] Soviet diplomats in Vienna said that "non-alignment is not for socialism," as reported by the Yugoslav ambassador to Moscow.[33] Yugoslav–Arab relations deteriorated in all those cases where Soviet bilateral aid to those countries was substantial.

Yugoslav–Soviet relations continued to observe a high frequency of mutual contacts, but suspicion remained and even grew. They talked, cooperated, traded, but there was no good faith or trust between the two countries. Tito visited the U.S.S.R. again in 1973, talking with the Soviet leadership for four days. Along with the statement that Tito "preserved our independence; he did not enter the CMEA, nor the Warsaw Pact," the conclusion of the meeting was that Tito was the "organizer and initiator of the concept of non-alignment," which pulled the whole world of the non-aligned from "the reserve of capitalism to the reserve of socialism, naturally the self-governing kind," which were "the true principles of non-alignment."[34]

The well-informed Ivan Buković wrote similarly in 1974, when Speaker of the Parliament of the Socialist Republic of Croatia Jakov Blažević informed him about "confidential information from the Presidency of the SFRY." The East German government had invited all military attachés for consultations. The development of the situation in Yugoslavia had to be monitored because further strengthening of the centralist government could strengthen separatism once Tito was gone. "This means that the brothers are preparing to intervene," the senior Croatian politician commented in his journal.[35] Some of the generals of the JNA were "a direct link to the Soviet intelligence service": Radojica Nenezić, Mirko Bulović, and the politician Dušan Čalić. Nenezić and Bulović were suspended as Soviet agents, and some lower-ranking officers were arrested. In the summer of 1974, "the Soviets organized a grand cleansing in Hungary. Ministers are killing themselves. One fell into the red-hot steel in a steel mill. Resignations are being tendered [...] The Soviets hold their world firmly in their hands."[36] Edvard Kardelj, Yugoslavia's number two, spent nine days in Moscow, Novosibirsk, and Bratsk from 1 to 10 September 1974. In October 1974, *Krasnaya Zvezda*, the official newspaper of the Soviet Ministry of Defense, censored several of Tito's replies in an interview, but the Yugoslav side did not make an issue out of the incident, although they did not invite Soviet Ambassador to Belgrade Stëpakov for an interview, even though there were such proposals.[37] Far more

---

32 Mićunović, *Moskovske godine*, 83–84.
33 Izvještaj političkog aktiva, in Buković Ćiro, diary, 22 June 1971.
34 Buković Ćiro, diary, 15 September 1973.
35 Ibid., 10 April 1974.
36 Ibid., 3 July 1974.
37 Mandić, *S Titom*, 56–57.

serious was the attempt to establish the Communist Party of Yugoslavia, one that was supposed to build true communism, a path that had been interrupted in 1948.[38] Soviet diplomats were also involved in this. Comments by Yugoslav officials about the 1976 Communist Party congresses in Sofia and Prague were similar to those of the 1950s: "Bulgarians and Czechoslovaks hold their congresses. These are no longer national parties. Blindly, under the pretext of internationalism, these parties serve the interests of Greater Russia, or more precisely the U.S.S.R."[39] This was exactly where the LCY and Yugoslavia differed from the countries of the Warsaw Pact and they wanted to preserve that status.

Yugoslav politicians often referred to the Soviets in their disputes. In October 1975, relations were described as "somewhere between cold and icy with a tendency to deteriorate further, but – of course – with a question mark at the end."[40] In his diary, Buković noted sentences he exchanged with his colleagues: "You want a general commotion and the Russians behind it."[41] "What these over-the-top Soviet communists are doing is a disgrace." "The Russians are attacking us more and more." "Don't you know," Dušan Bilandžić, a member of the Croatian League of Communists Central Committee, told Buković in 1976, "that the Russians really want to break up Yugoslavia. They would like to split Yugoslavia up into six independent republics and then link them to the greater U.S.S.R. together with Bulgaria."[42] Despite such considerations and all the barely concealed doubts about the sincerity of the Soviet leadership, Federal Foreign Minister Miloš Minić visited Moscow in 1975 and 1978. Brezhnev went to Yugoslavia in 1975. Tito then visited Moscow in 1977 on the anniversary of the October Revolution, and again in 1979.[43]

Tito's illness caused new difficulties. In relation to the intervention in Afghanistan, additional military activity was observed in neighboring countries, even in those belonging to the Warsaw Pact. The forces of the Red Army had been grouping in Hungary, and ferry traffic toward the Bulgarian port of Varna had increased. In the end, nothing happened. Viewed from outside, Yugoslavia was strong enough; on the inside, all who expected difficulties understood the situation only too well, but the time for disintegration had not come yet.[44]

---

38 Ivo Banac, *Sa Staljinom protiv Tita, Informbirovski rascjepi u jugoslavenskom komunističkom pokretu* (Zagreb: Globus, 1990), 248.
39 Buković Ćiro, diary, 11 April 1976; 7 April 1974.
40 Tuđman, *"Osobni dnevnik 1,"* 9 November 1975, 210.
41 Buković Ćiro, diary, 25 April 1978.
42 Ibid., 30 August 1978; 18 May 1976.
43 Mandić, *Tito u dijalogu*, 514–21; 632–38.
44 Branko Mamula, *Slučaj Jugoslavija* (Beograd: Dan Graf i Plus, 2014), 34.

Figure 2: Leonid Brezhnev in a conversation with Josip Broz Tito at the White Palace in Belgrade (Source: Keystone Press / Alamy Stock Photo)

V. Non-alignment as a guarantee of the future

For Yugoslavia, détente was a period of successful resolution of important and long-standing unresolved relations with a number of neighboring countries. The beginning of the Helsinki Process and the Conference on European Security and Cooperation institutionalized non-alignment on the Old Continent. Three European countries, the SFRY, Cyprus, and Malta, which became a permanent member of the Movement in 1973,[45] now formed a visible, Mediterranean, non-aligned bloc. By the end of the decade of détente, a group of neutral and non-aligned countries, the NN group, had been fully institutionalized. (Other members were Sweden, Finland, Switzerland, Austria, Lichtenstein and San Marino). They had limited influence on the overall relations between the West and the East, but they helped overcome the stalemate on the Continent between the two opposing blocks. Yugoslavia's active role in the Helsinki process, speeded up the

---

45 Berislav Badurina, *Alžirska konferencija* (Beograd:IP "Rad", 1975), 4.

tional relations."⁵¹ Yugoslav opposition to Cuba and all countries in the NAM that were closer to Soviet views was the best that could be achieved within the existing framework. This was not a Western position, but it was not an Eastern policy either, and in that sense it is quite clear how acceptable the Yugoslav approach was. At the very end of the era, a few days before the Soviet intervention in Afghanistan, the U.S. ambassador to Belgrade, later Secretary of State Lawrence Eagleburger, pointed out that non-alignment was "crucial" for Yugoslavia. It was a policy by which the SFRY remained independent of the blocs.

Yugoslav policies in the NAM, as well as the resolutions passed, were often harsh toward the West, but were clearly far more acceptable than possible resolutions that would have been drawn up by other contenders for leadership in the Third World. Non-acceptance or insufficient valorization of the Yugoslav non-aligned orientation was beginning to be considered unacceptable, almost offensive. Non-alignment was a foreign policy doctrine. To negate this was to negate the very foundations of the Yugoslav Federation. Yugoslavia saw the principles of the Movement as a desirable foreign policy orientation toward both the West and the East, but as especially useful to Belgrade. All this had to suit everyone who was against radicalization in international relations.

The 1973 conference in Algeria was strongly oriented around exploitation policies, the rage of the undeveloped who lagged behind in development, despite great wealth. "We have now prevented these extremes in Algeria, but I am not sure that this can be prevented for a long time, unless you rich people come to your senses," Tito said in late September 1973 in negotiations with British MPs.⁵² There was a lot of power among the non-aligned countries, and the states that were seemingly the favorites of the West did not require much persuasion to invest in the Fund for the Development of the Undeveloped – countries such as Saudi Arabia, Kuwait, and then Libya.

High-ranking Yugoslav politicians later recounted how Tito called Algerian President Houari Boumédièn to "reason" with him, to persuade him not to clash with Morocco and Egypt at the Conference of Ministers of the Non-Aligned.⁵³ Yugoslavia often mediated because it had excellent relations with all Arab countries, which was never good enough for the United States, but was far below what the Soviet leadership expected. During the Sixth Conference in Cuba in 1979, the Yugoslav reaction to Castro's policies may not have been strong enough, but it was crucial if "the line of the natural alliance of the non-aligned countries with the countries of the Soviet bloc were to fail." Egypt, which had just

---

51 Zabilješka o razgovoru saveznog sekretara za vanjske poslove Josipa Vrhovca sa državnim sekretarom SAD Sajrus Vensom, u Njujorku 26. septembra 1978. godine, SSIP, Josip Vrhovec's personal collection, Zagreb.
52 Buković Ćiro, diary, 24 September 1973; Dinkel, *The Non-aligned Movement*, 146–151.
53 Buković Ćiro, diary, 25 July 1978.

signed an agreement in Camp David, was expelled from the Arab League. The Arabs also wanted to eject Egypt from NAM, but Yugoslavia was insistent that it should remain within the Movement. The Egyptians had not even sent their foreign minister to Havana. Instead, the number two in their diplomatic service, Boutros Boutros-Ghali went to avoid attempts to humiliate his country. Yugoslavia thus saved Egypt from being excluded from the Movement. This was undoubtedly in the interests of peace and indirectly beneficial to the West and Israel.[54] It meant that the Yugoslav position was far more open, but also broad enough to retain the whole movement on "original principles," which provided a position the blocs could live with while Yugoslavia could ensure its national policy and dominance in the Movement.

Before Mikhail Gorbachev came to power, the Soviet Union did not accept a separate path to socialism, even in relation to the policy of non-alignment, but merely tolerated it. The Non-Aligned Movement was ignored by the Soviet Union, which caused great irritation in Belgrade. At the twenty-fifth Congress of the KPSS in 1976, of which Ivan Buković was informed as a member of the Federation Council, the leader of the Yugoslav delegation, Stane Dolanc, complained that the formal host of the LCY, Andrei Gromyko, was never present at formal lunches with the Yugoslavs. Brezhnev never mentioned the non-aligned in his paper, and there was little of substance to his "lukewarm" speech. Miloš Minić, the Yugoslav Federal Secretary of State for Foreign Affairs, asked Gromyko the reason for such behavior. The Soviet minister first argued "arrogantly", that it had been mentioned, but when faced with the facts, he admitted that everything "was cut due to length." Then, according to Dolanc, he retorted: "We are for your Non-Aligned Movement if it stands firmly on the anti-imperialist course. However, you also have in your camp people like Mobutu [the president of Zaire], who is a servant to the imperialists. ... We support you, but you have to turn the Non-Aligned Movement into a course of anti-imperialism.' Dolanc snapped. 'We have had enough of your patronizing. What do you have to tell us about anti-imperialism? We have done more to snatch the UN away from the hands of the imperialists, and especially the Americans, than you could ever do with your policy. ... Don't you have Mobutu in your camp?' Gromyko started angry, insulted."[55] Was it not foolish to fail to invite to the Congress the FLN from Algeria, which led the revolution, or the decision to invite the Ba'ath Party, which was building socialism in Iraq while communist politicians were being imprisoned? Truth be told, the Yugoslavs also expressed their dissatisfaction with

---

54 Aktivnost L. Eagleburger, ambasadora SAD u SFRJ, SSIP, Ambasada SFRJ Washington, br. 992, 12 December 1979, Josip Vrhovec's personal collection, Zagreb; Tvrtko Jakovina, *Treća strana Hladnog rata*. 192, 224–225.
55 Buković Ćiro, diary, 14 April 1976; Dinkel, *The Non-aligned Movement*, 215.

all those representatives of the NAM who also failed to mention the Movement. Dolanc saved his most vehement attack for the North Koreans. "We had to cut it short, so we left it out," they told him. The Soviet representatives then demanded that the reference to the Moscow and Belgrade declarations be removed from the final declaration, that their own path to socialism not be mentioned anywhere, and that the term "non-aligned" be removed. Yugoslav politicians then sent a telegram to Tito, proposing that the LCY withdraw from the congress, after which everything died down. The Soviet team acted as if nothing had happened, apparently familiar with the content of the message to Belgrade, and once again became convinced of the resolute position of the Yugoslav delegation.

Brezhnev's letter to the Yugoslav head of state before the Fifth Conference of the NAM in Colombo in 1976 was also a kind of pressure, as the Soviet leader expressed hope that Yugoslavia would set the Movement "on an anti-imperialist course." Tito responded to this by addressing the Yugoslav public. For Yugoslavia, non-alignment was a natural course of the development of the human race. Precisely because of its own ideology, Yugoslavia had just pushed the entire orientation, channeling it. The differences among the non-aligned countries were not in themselves problematic, but the behavior of those who insisted on them was. The Non-Aligned Movement could not serve as a preserve of superpowers and their policies.[56] The Soviet Union was constantly striving for "the non-aligned to unilaterally attack American imperialism and leave room for their variant of imperialism camouflaged by 'proletarian internationalism'."[57] Belgrade could recognize such a danger more easily than many other countries. Positioning itself between Soviet "hegemony" and Western "imperialism" was the Yugoslav mantra and philosophy with which they guided the Non-Aligned Movement.

VI. Conclusion – Danger from where?

When the European threats to Yugoslavia largely subsided, when after Stalin's death in 1953 it became clear that Soviet intervention was not inevitable, and also when it became clear that the change in the Yugoslav course could not be considered temporary, the country really became non-aligned in the true sense of the word. It was a huge step forward for a country that sought its own foreign policy path and strove to continue to be able to stress its own uniqueness, willing to draw attention to its own position. It was in Yugoslavia's interest to ease the tensions between Moscow and Belgrade without spoiling good relations with

---

56 Buković Ćiro, diary, 31 July 1976.
57 Ibid., 23 August 1976.

Washington. This left room for action outside the European framework, in the Non-Aligned Movement, where Yugoslavia advocated ideas that suited most Third World countries, especially those that did not want conflict with either of the superpowers and yet wanted neither the continuation of neocolonial Western domination nor the "proletarian internationalism" or "hegemony" of the Soviet Union. This made Yugoslavia present and active, although it took a long time to close the gap between the general acceptance within the NAM and its leaders and the positions of the superpowers, which showed misunderstanding, rejection, and even complete disparagement of Yugoslavia's main foreign policy orientation – permanently (in the case of the Soviet Union) or for a very long time (in the case of the U.S.).

Objectively, the Soviet Union was the main real threat to Yugoslav integrity, but good relations with the United States, as well as improving relations with China, considerable armed forces, and a clear attitude toward Moscow on the part of the SFRY leadership were sufficient protection. No one would provoke a global conflict because of potential aggression toward Yugoslavia, which could only come from the East, just as no one would do so over of Berlin. The Yugoslavs were aware of this. The Yugoslav Federation could rely on the help and sympathy of many, but only a willingness to offer resistance internally while exerting influence internationally and the possibility of internationalizing its own position, could provide more lasting defense.

The FPRY had used internationalization for its own defense since the severance of relations with the Soviet Union in 1948. Through the UN, it kept protesting loudly and warning of Stalin's aggressive policies. It later became an element of its foreign policy, and the only forums where the Yugoslav voice could be heard were multilateral organizations, primarily the UN. The Non-Aligned Movement was a forum in which Yugoslavia qualified as a spokesman for the Third World. As the most active NAM country, it was able to assert its importance and increase its influence by advocating principles that were acceptable to many in the Third World, but especially at home in Yugoslavia. When Prince Norodom Sihanouk of Cambodia came to Brijuni to visit Tito on 12 June 1973, he declared, "In the world, Yugoslavia is a country to whose attitude one reacts." "Tito is a wonderful and influential person in the world," he praised his host.[58] At the conference in Colombo in 1976, the Tunisian foreign minister conveyed a message from Habib Bourguiba, the ailing head of state, asking that Tito personally represent him. "Since you are the father of the non-alignment policy, you have to take care of your children, who continue to grow."[59] Such ideas strengthened

---

58 Buković Ćiro, diary, 12 June 1973.
59 Mandić, *S Titom*, 221.

Yugoslav self-confidence. It was for this reason that non-alignment became a doctrine, one of the pillars on which the Yugoslav state rested.

Détente accelerated all Yugoslav foreign policies and helped Yugoslavia achieve a number of foreign policy goals. Some of them did not have the most direct connection to what Yugoslavia managed to do in Lusaka in 1970 or Havana in 1979, but they were not always unrelated to what Belgrade did in the Third World. The border agreement with Italy was once linked to Yugoslavia's rapprochement with Ethiopia, just as rapprochement with China was interpreted as China's desire to join the NAM, at least in Albania. For Yugoslavia, détente was actually the best of all periods. All the policies it advocated became (declaratively) accepted both in Europe and by the superpowers. This position made Yugoslavia a visible, morally correct, and acceptable interlocutor in various circles.

With the end of the Cold War, Yugoslavia began to lose its external framework, which strengthened the country; all the foreign policy achievements, which mainly occurred in the era of détente, continued even without Tito, and grew toward the end of the following decade, primarily in the context of more sincere relations with the Soviet Union under Mikhail Gorbachev. Viewed from the outside, Yugoslavia appeared to be strong; it had achieved reconciliation with most of its neighbors, and its borders were set. However, it disintegrated from within, despite strong armed forces and the fact that it chaired the ninth NAM Conference in 1989, which was then welcomed by almost everyone. Circumstances within a country are sometimes more influenced by football fans and their gangs than the praise of the German or the U.S. secretaries of state. This was precisely the case in the European Southeast in 1991.

Effie G. H. Pedaliu

The United States, Differentiation, and Balkan Cooperation during the Cold War

I.   Introduction

"As an international system the Cold War was riddled with contradictions," concedes Arne Westad.[1] The Cold War divided the Balkan peninsula along ideological lines, but the region soon emerged as a location for converging strategic dilemmas. The Balkan states's enduring preoccupation with national borders was thwarted by the awe-inspiring Cold War frontline that dissected it. Tito's Yugoslavia opted for a policy of equidistance from the superpowers, which introduced ambivalence and prevented the establishment of neat division. The Cold War purportedly enabled Greece to escape the tyranny of its geography and become, politically and even culturally, non-Balkan. The dislocation was even greater for Turkey, displaced from both the Balkans and the Middle East. The Cold War did not impede the superpowers in testing each other's resolve or sowing discord in each other's sphere of influence. The hunger for development in the Balkans offered the United States the opportunity to "hone in on" the instrument of "differentiation"[2] that was an integral feature of containment from 1949 on and was bequeathed by each Cold War U.S. president to his successor. It aimed to exacerbate imperceptibly any tensions in the Soviet bloc, by rewarding, primarily through trade, Eastern European countries that manifested signs of independence from the U.S.S.R or made moves towards internal liberalization.[3]

This essay looks at the role of the Balkan peninsula in U.S. Cold War policy and examines the effects of differentiation on local developments and the evolution of the Cold War. It uses the term "the Balkans" as the collective noun for the region, the term used by most who hail from it. For all the stereotypical images it may

---

[1] Odd Arne Westad, "The Balkans: A Cold War Mystery," in *The Balkans in the Cold War,* edited by Svetozar Rajak et al. (London: Palgrave Macmillan, 2017), 355–362.
[2] Effie G. H. Pedaliu, "The US, the Balkans and Détente," in *The Balkans in the Cold War,* edited by Svetozar Rajak et al. (London: Palgrave Macmillan, 2017), 197–218.
[3] *Foreign Relations of the United States* (*FRUS*) 1949, Volume V: *Eastern Europe; The Soviet Union* (Washington, D.C.: United States Government Printing Office, 1975), document 10.

invoke, it defines the region not just as a space for internecine nationalist conflict but also as a space for seeking cooperation in the form of a "Balkan Federation" or "Balkan Union" stretching from "the Alps to Cyprus" – efforts that were undertaken not only by socialists and communists, but also by liberal internationalists.[4] To reject it in favour of a deliberately evasive and opaque geographical term such as Southeastern Europe, could promote the stereotypes it intends to avoid as well as ahistorical approaches to the study of the region and, in the long run, historical amnesia.[5]

II. The Legacy of WWII

Liberation found Balkan societies deeply divided and seeking divergent political futures. Total war, collaboration, resistance and survival had become intertwined with pre-existing disputes and regional competition. Nazi Germany's and Fascist Italy's conquests were accompanied by energetic occupations by the "puppet" governments of Bulgaria, Hungary, and Romania and had created a combustible security environment. The Soviet Union's success in pushing Hitler' armies westward appealed to popular mood in the occupied Balkans more than the slower-moving Anglo-American strategy that aimed to divert Nazi Germany away from reinforcing the shores of France.[6] Allied "grand strategy" in the Balkans was experienced as a clamp that increased the ferocity of occupation, intensified disunity, and bifurcated local resistance into communist and anti-communist groupings. It bred frustration and fostered suspicion. The cynicism evinced by the Stalin–Churchill percentages agreement in 1944 anticipated a

---

4 Leften Stavrianos, *Balkan Federation: A History of the Movement Toward Balkan Unity in Modern Times* (Hamden: Archon Books, 1964); Francesca Gori and Silvio Pons (eds.), *The Soviet Union and Europe in the Cold War, 1943–53* (London: Palgrave Macmillan, 1996), 125–35; Alexandros Papanastassiou, *Vers l'union balkanique* (Paris: La Conciliation Internationale, 1934).

5 Pamela Ballinger, *History in Exile: Memory and Identity at the Borders of the Balkans* (Princeton: Princeton University Press, 2003); Alex Drace-Francis, "The Prehistory of a Neologism: 'South-Eastern Europe'," *Balkanologie: Revue d'études pluridisciplinaires* 3 (1999) 2: 1–10; Paschalis Kitromilides, "Imagined Communities and the Origin of the National Question in the Balkans," *European History Quarterly* 19 (1989) 2: 149–94; Mark Mazower, *The Balkans* (London: Phoenix Paperback, 2000); Maria N. Todorova, *Imagining the Balkans* (Oxford: Oxford University Press, 1997), 27–30, 46.

6 Michael Howard, *The Mediterranean Strategy in the Second World War* (New York: Praeger, 1968), 42, 70; Matthew Jones, *Britain, the United States and the Mediterranean War, 1942–44* (London: Macmillan Press, 1996), 99–100; Paolo Fonzi, "'Beyond the Myth of the 'Good Italian': Recent Trends in the Study of the Italian Occupation of Southeastern Europe during the Second World War," *Südosteuropa* 65 (2017) 2: 239–59.

future based on division.[7] It also revealed that American opposition to spheres of influence was flexible. In Athens, the December Events demonstrated that Britain, starved of the resources it needed to finance its postwar strategy, could resort to heavy-handedness to avert communist takeovers.[8] In the Balkans, the shape of peace had been imagined in a multiplicity of ways and was contested before it had even arrived. The communists were convinced that the future belonged to them and nationalists were equally determined to prove them wrong.

III. From Total War to Cold War

The Cold War did not begin over the Balkans, but Cold War tensions manifested there and in neighboring Italy earlier than in other parts of Europe. Peace finally arrived only when the United States intervened and the Soviet Union restrained its proxies. For this to happen, both superpowers had to come to terms with their new status as the hegemons of two antagonistic blocs. The United States revised its dismissive attitude to Balkan and Eastern Mediterranean matters once it came to view these through the lens of a looming geopolitical conflict.[9] The Mediterranean Sea emerged as an arena of competition over ideology and energy resources, and its significance for Western security was upgraded. U.S. foreign policy makers had to ascertain how developments in the Balkans could affect the security of Italy, the Eastern Mediterranean and wider American interests in the region.[10] By early 1945, the United States recognized that the political situation in Italy was fluid and that, because of British weakness, it had to assume responsibility for the country's reconstruction. Italian instability raised the prospect that civil war could spread westwards from Greece, destabilizing the whole of

---

7 Albert Resis, "The Churchill-Stalin Secret 'Percentages' Agreement on the Balkans, Moscow, October 1944," *American Historical Review* 83 (1978) 2: 368–87; Eduard Mark, "American Policy Toward Eastern Europe and the Origins of the Cold War, 1941–1946: An Alternative Interpretation," *The Journal of American History*, 68 (1981) 2: 313–36.
8 John O. Iatrides, *Revolt in Athens: The Greek Communist "Second Round," 1944–1945* (Princeton: Princeton University Press, 1972); Mark Mazower (ed.), *After the War Was Over: Reconstructing the Family, Nation, and State in Greece, 1943–1960* (Princeton: Princeton University Press, 2000), 24–41; Panagiotis Delis, "The British Intervention in Greece: The Battle of Athens, December 1944," *Journal of Modern Greek Studies* 35 (2017) 1: 211–37; Leften Stavrianos, "Two Points of View: The Immediate Origins of the Battle of Athens," *American Slavic and East European Review* 8 (1949) 4: 239–51.
9 John O. Iatrides (ed.), *Ambassador MacVeagh Reports: Greece, 1933–1947* (New Jersey: Princeton University Press, 1980).
10 Geoff Swain, "The Cominform: Tito's International?" *The Historical Journal* 35 (1992) 3: 641–63; John O. Iatrides and Nicholas X. Rizopoulos, "The International Dimension of the Greek Civil War," *World Policy Journal* 17 (2000) 1: 87–103.

Europe. The events at Venezia Giulia in March 1945[11] in conjunction with the menacing and parallel Yugoslav territorial claims against the Austrian provinces of Carinthia and Styria[12] and Tito's obvious eyeing of Greek Macedonia led the United States to conclude that Yugoslav regional hegemonism was not wholly devoid of Soviet input.[13] By 1946, the Americans came to view the Balkans as a Soviet stepping stone to Western Europe that could also undermine the security of Greece, Turkey, Yugoslavia, Italy, and the Middle East. The Truman Doctrine and the Marshall Plan frustrated Soviet strategy towards Greece and Turkey. Stalin would not risk direct conflict with the United States or jeopardize Soviet gains in Eastern Europe for the sakes of the Southern European communists, so, he accepted the new architecture of the Balkans as it emerged after the Tito-Stalin split in 1948 and the defeat of the Greek Communists. He also made clear that the Soviet Union was unwilling to accommodate endless squabbling over borders within its bloc.[14]

The Cold War frontline in the Balkan peninsula was "secondary" or "peripheral" to the superpowers only in contrast to the ultimate Cold War border, the Central Front. This did not, however, make it negotiable. The expansion of NATO in 1952 to include Greece and Turkey and the establishment of the Warsaw Pact in 1955 meant that the "South Region" of the Warsaw Pact and the "Southern Flank" of NATO coincided in the Balkans. Both Moscow and Washington realized that it was in their interest to maintain the post-WWII status quo by controlling their allies' nationalistic impulses and keeping them in line. Over

---

11 Marina Cattaruzza, *Italy and its Eastern Border, 1866–2016* (New York: Routledge, 2017); Robert E. Niebuhr, *The Search for Cold War Legitimacy: Foreign Policy and Tito's Yugoslavia* (Boston: Brill, 2018); Bogdan C. Novak, *Trieste, 1941–1954: The Ethnic, Political, and Ideological Struggle* (Chicago: University of Chicago Press, 1970); Roberto G. Rabel, *Between East and West: Trieste, the United States, and the Cold War, 1941–1954* (Durham: Duke University Press, 1988).

12 Robert Knight, "Ethnicity and Identity in the Cold War: The Carinthian Border Dispute, 1945–1946," *International History Review* 22 (2000) 2: 274–303; Dušan Biber, "Yugoslav and British Policy towards the Carinthian Question, 1941–5," in *The Phoney Peace: Power and Culture in Central Europe 1945–49*, edited by Robert B. Pynsent, 100–12, <https://discovery.ucl.ac.uk/id/eprint/10078356/3/SSEES0021.pdf> (2 March 2021).

13 Jeronim Perović, "The Tito–Stalin Split: A Reassessment in Light of New Evidence," *Journal of Cold War Studies* 9 (2007) 2: 32–63; Svetozar Rajak, "No Bargaining Chips, No Spheres of Interest: The Yugoslav Origins of Cold War Non-Alignment," *Journal of Cold War Studies* 16 (2014) 1: 146–79.

14 Geoffrey Roberts, "Moscow's Cold War on the Periphery: Soviet Policy in Greece, Iran, and Turkey, 1943–8," *Journal of Contemporary History* 46 (2011) 1: 58–81; Vladislav M. Zubok, *A Failed Empire: The Soviet Union in the Cold War from Stalin to Gorbachev* (Chapel Hill: The University of North Carolina Press, 2009), 38–9; Mark Kramer, "Stalin, Soviet Policy, and the Establishment of a Communist Bloc in Eastern Europe, 1941–1948," in *Stalin and Europe: Imitation and Domination, 1928–1953*, edited by Timothy Snyder and Ray Brandon (Oxford: Oxford University Press, 2014), 264–94.

time, the Cold War seemed have helped to keep "uncharacteristically calm" a region where ambitions to correlate national borders with national identities had remained unmet since the collapse of the Ottoman Empire.[15] Stability came at the cost of division, compromised sovereignty, and the hasty cloaking of identity politics into wider ideological constructs. All, increased unpredictability.

For the war-ravaged Balkan states, the Cold War meant both regression and transformation. Great power competition and familiar clientelistic relations returned but also turned the region from a backwater into a frontline. The Graeco-Bulgarian border, as Evanthis Hatzivassiliou has demonstrated, remained prone to skirmishes that could draw in the superpowers. At the Paris Peace Conference in 1946, Greece, with civil war still raging and having suffered three Bulgarian invasions, sought borders that afforded security from its intrusive neighbor.[16] Theodora Dragostinova has shown how Bulgarian insistence on borders providing Bulgaria economic advantage involved control of areas disputed by Greece. Problems also arose between Bulgaria and Yugoslavia over the borders of the People's Republic of Macedonia. The two countries were able to settle some of their differences in 1946, but Moscow had to intervene.[17] Albania grew distrustful of its neighbors and hegemons alike. In the Balkans, nationalism remained alive on both sides of the Cold War divide. Kapka Kassabova has described this pervasive distrust on the Balkan frontline beautifully: "the Turks were nervous about the Soviets and the Greeks, the Greeks were nervous about the Soviets and the Turks, and the Bulgarians were nervous about everyone."[18]

IV. America and the Balkans during the 'High Cold War'

America was drawn into the Balkans reluctantly. The region remained one of secondary importance, but American strategists could hardly ignore that Soviet lines of communication to the Mediterranean ran through the Balkans, especially with Albania offering basal facilities until 1962. Any American policy towards the region would be complex. The various communist Balkan states chose different paths to achieving socialism and each posed unique security considerations. The

---

15 Directorate of Intelligence, Instability in the Balkans, 15 June 1983, CIA/(FOIA)/ESDN (CREST): CIA-RDP85T00287R000501610001-0.
16 Evanthis Hatzivassiliou, "Negotiating with the enemy: the normalization of Greek-Bulgarian relations, 1960–1964," *Southeast European and Black Sea Studies* 4 (2004) 1: 140–61; Evanthis Hatzivassiliou, "Security and the European Option: Greek Foreign Policy, 1952–62," *Journal of Contemporary History* 30 (1995) 1: 187–202.
17 Theodora Dragostinova, "On 'Strategic Frontiers': Debating the Borders of the Post-Second World War Balkans," *Contemporary European History* 27 (2018) 3: 387–411.
18 Kapka Kassabova, *Border: A Journey to the End of Europe* (Minneapolis: Graywolf Press, 2017).

U.S. was hampered by restricted information and intelligence. Within this environment, two major concerns prevailed, namely preventing Soviet power from spilling south and developing an ability to reach behind the "Iron Curtain" in a way that did not provoke major war.[19]

The region offered unique terrain. Its diversity appeared to represent a model of the looming bipolar conflict; it would enable the United States to better adapt containment to weaken "Soviet Communism" and assess the limits of brinkmanship under the relative opacity of the alarm the Greek Civil War was generating. From 1946 to 1949, the United States gained clear indications of the efficacy, limitations, and potential of containment. There was a palpable sense that its methods could lead to victory when Yugoslavia flipped. The Tito-Stalin split of 1948 lessened Italian defensive vulnerability from the Ljubljana Gap and made the Greek Civil War more manageable. Above all, it represented a minute yet significant 'roll-back' of Soviet power. From 1949, "keeping Tito afloat" by extending political and economic support to Yugoslavia enabled the United States to set out its stall of alternatives to the Soviet satellites.[20]

The "loss" of Albania and Bulgaria in the late 1940s did not come about due to a lack of effort, but was accepted after a reassessment of American capabilities and strategic priorities. The long-term lessons were that policy objectives and exit strategies needed to be carefully calibrated. Practical information was gained on how long dissent could survive under systematic state persecution and when to cut aid and contact with dissident movements.[21] The CIA's first major joint operation with the British against Albania, codenamed Operation BG/FIEND, began in June 1949, a few months before the end of the Greek Civil War, and lasted, intermittently, until 1953. It resulted in the destruction of anti-communist Albanian networks that had been compromised from the start and it provided the newly minted CIA with invaluable insights as to how to approach future covert operations. The unfathomable betrayal exposed by this operation was to shape the United States' emotional understanding of the conflict, the enemy and eventually, its allies.[22]

---

19 Dionysios Chourchoulis, *The Southern Flank of NATO, 1951–1959: Military Strategy or Political Stabilization* (Lanham: Lexington Books, 2014).
20 Lorraine M. Lees, *Keeping Tito Afloat: The United States, Yugoslavia, and the Cold War* (University Park: Pennsylvania State University Press, 1997).
21 Michael M. Boll, *Cold War in the Balkans: American Policy towards Bulgaria 1943–1947* (Lexington: UP of Kentucky, 1984); Vesselin Dimitrov, *Stalin's Cold War: Soviet Foreign Policy, Democracy and Communism in Bulgaria, 1941–48* (London: Palgrave Macmillan, 2008); Vasil Paraskevov, "Conflict and necessity: British–Bulgarian relations, 1944–56," *Cold War History* 11 (2011) 2: 241–68.
22 James Callanan, *Covert Action in the Cold War: US Intelligence and CIA Operations* (London: I. B. Tauris, 2009), 73, 77, 78, 80; Albert Lulushi, *Operation Valuable Fiend: The CIA's First Paramilitary Strike Against the Iron Curtain* (New York: Arcade Publishing, 2014); Stephen

Bulgaria made President Truman realize the limits to diplomacy and power.[23] In the mid to late 1940s, American economic interests in Bulgaria experienced relentless hostility, and embassy staff in Sofia suffered systematic persecution. The point of no return was reached with the show trial of the former general secretary of the Bulgarian Communist Party, Traicho Kostov, who was accused of collusion with Tito. No sooner had the U.S. ambassador to Bulgaria, Ronald R. Heath, reported that "Titoism" was not "a significant political force in Bulgaria"[24] than he found himself framed, embroiled in the Kostov indictment, and declared *persona non grata*. Truman closed the embassy, suspecting that the Bulgarians would not have dared to push matters so far without Moscow's approval. His suspension of diplomatic relations with Bulgaria was designed to send the U.S.S.R. a shot across the bows.[25]

Greece and Turkey were also assigned special roles. As Larry Kaplan put it, Greece was identified as "an arena of international conflict" and Turkey as "a barrier."[26] The elevation of the strategic value of both countries into valuable bricks in the wall of containment via the Truman Doctrine and the Marshall Plan embedded them into the "free world." The ferocity unleashed in August 1949, during the final clashes of the Greek Civil War, on Mount Grammos, served as a demonstration of America's firepower and underscored that this was a line not to be crossed. Two months later, General James Van Fleet, the Director of the Joint United States Military, Advisory and Planning Group in Greece mooted rolling back "the iron curtain still farther in the Balkans."[27] With the end of the Greek Civil War and the solidifying of the "Iron Curtain," U.S. policy towards the Balkans settled into a blend of caution mixed with dynamic adventurism. Holding the line and keeping the balance of power stable did not preclude probing or economic and commercial exchange. Despite the passing of the Export Control Act in 1949, economic warfare and economic statecraft went hand in hand in U.S. Cold War foreign strategy."[28]

Through its newly established National Security institutions as well as the Voice of America and Radio Free Europe (RFE), the Truman administration

---

Long, "CIA-MI6 psychological warfare and the subversion of communist Albania in the early Cold War," *Intelligence and National Security* 35 (2020) 6: 787–807.

23 Annual Message to the Congress on the State of the Union, 7 January 1948, in *Public Papers of the Presidents of the US, Harry S. Truman, 1 January to 31 December 1948* (Washington DC: Office of the Federal Register, NARA, 1948), 7.
24 *FRUS* 1949, V, document 219.
25 Ibid., document 206.
26 Lawrence S. Kaplan, *A Community of Interests: NATO and the Military Assistance Program, 1948–1951* (Washington DC: Office of the Secretary of Defence, 1980), 4–7.
27 *FRUS* 1949, Volume VI: *The Near East, South Asia, and Africa* (Washington, D.C.: United States Government Printing Office, 1977), document 249.
28 *FRUS* 1949, V, document 10.

attempted to reach hearts and minds behind the "Iron Curtain." If containment appeared to be static on Truman's watch, this was because those who calibrated the message were prudent in their pledges. Clear instructions had been issued not to 'promise imminent liberation or encourage active revolt."[29] In the Balkans, "roll-back'" and "differentiation" as permutations of containment were evident from the late 1940s. The United States had the opportunity to trial more safely than elsewhere in Europe the precepts of NSC 58/2, namely to seek "the gradual reduction and eventual elimination of preponderant Soviet power from Eastern Europe without resort to war; [...] through fostering Communist heresy among the satellite states."[30] Eastern Europe remained the big prize, but the Balkans were essential in shaping the guidelines of NSC 58/2 and for the conclusion – enduring throughout the Cold War – that trade was the best means available to make U.S. influence "most concretely [...] felt" behind the "Iron Curtain."[31]

The "Cold War Respite" provided by Stalin's death facilitated the convening of the Geneva Conference in 1955.[32] "The spirit of Geneva" ran out of steam as the German issue remained intractable and Khrushchev trained his sights on the Third World. President Eisenhower's version of détente, combining the relaxation of tensions alongside active psychological warfare, had reached as far as it could go in the face of Soviet intransigence over "verification." By 1956, the limits to any "roll-back" by "liberation" in Eastern Europe without direct Western involvement had been exposed twice – in East Germany in 1953 and in Hungary in 1956. After the United States reconsidered its policy towards Eastern Europe, it adopted NSC-5811/1, which recommended the expansion of "non-strategic trade with the Soviet-dominated nations for primarily political purposes."[33]

In this climate, differentiation was customized to be applied individually towards Eastern European countries.[34] In the Balkans, the fermentation of nationalism as a means of "accelerating evolution towards independence from Soviet control" took primacy over the promotion of internal change. The main tools of the policy would be economic and cultural, but with the proviso that

---

29 *FRUS* 1950, Volume IV: *Central and Eastern Europe; The Soviet Union* (Washington, D.C.: United States Government Printing Office, 1980), document 8.
30 *FRUS* 1949, V, document 10.
31 Ibid.
32 Günter Bischof and Saki Dockrill (eds.), *Cold War Respite: The Geneva Summit of 1955* (Baton Rouge: Louisiana State University Press, 2000).
33 *FRUS* 1958–1960, Volume X, Part 1: *Eastern Europe Region; Soviet Union; Cyprus* (Washington, D.C.: United States Government Printing Office, 1993), document 5; Saki Dockrill, *Eisenhower's New Look National Security Policy, 1953–61* (London: Palgrave Macmillan, 1996).
34 *FRUS* 1958–1960, Volume X, Part 1, document 6.

these could not be construed as "stirring up" rebellion.[35] Albania's hostility to the United States and its fear of Greece, Italy, and Yugoslavia made it less amenable to any entreaties from the U.S.[36] Romania was judged to be a better candidate for cultivation[37] and Bulgaria would not be ignored. Since 1957, Bulgaria had been making positive noises about reengaging diplomatically with the United States and the latter suspected that the British were sharing only "filtered" information about developments in Sofia.[38] Secretary of State Christian Herter suggested that diplomatic relations be restored as soon as the Bulgarians retracted their charges of espionage against Heath.[39] An agreement on reestablishing diplomatic relations was arrived at in 1959, the U.S. embassy in Sofia reopened in 1960, and the issue of economic relations appeared on the horizon. Thus, the Eisenhower Administration bequeathed to its successors tense, but improving relations with the region.

V. JFK, the Balkans and "the art of playing the diffusion of power within the Communist world"

In 1961, differentiation and bluster met. For Nikita Khrushchev, "peaceful coexistence" came to signify "a form of intense economic, political and ideological struggle [...] in the international arena." On 6 January 1961, he welcomed the newly elected U.S. president by proclaiming the "liberation wars would continue to exist so long as imperialism exists," and that "peace cannot be begged for; it can only be assured by active purposeful struggle."[40] During his election campaign, John F. Kennedy promised that the United States would not forget Eastern Europeans nor agree to "any formal approval of the status quo."[41] He asked his transition team to rethink U.S. policy towards Eastern Europe and charged his

---

35 *FRUS* 1958–1960, Volume X, Part 2: *Eastern Europe; Finland; Greece; Turkey* (Washington, D.C.: United States Government Printing Office, 1993), documents 32, 33 and 34.
36 Ibid., document 31.
37 *FRUS* 1958–1960, X, Part 1, document 6.
38 Gregory Mitrovich, *Undermining the Kremlin: America's Strategy to Subvert the Soviet Bloc, 1947–1956* (Ithaca: Cornell University Press, 2000).
39 *FRUS* 1958–1960, X, Part 2, documents 31, 32, 34, 42.
40 Report by Nikita Khrushchev presented at the Institute of Marxism-Leninism in Moscow on 6 January 1961: "For New Victories of the World Communist Movement," 6 January 1961 <https://novaonline.nvcc.edu/eli/evans/HIS242/Documents/1961ConferenceReport.pdf> (1 July 2021).
41 A. Paul Kubricht, "Politics and Foreign Policy: A Brief Look at the Kennedy Administration's Eastern European Diplomacy," *Diplomatic History* 11 (1987) 1: 55–65.

secretary of state, Dean Rusk, with intensifying the "exchange of persons programs behind the 'Iron Curtain'."[42]

Kennedy's ability to advance differentiation meaningfully was to be disrupted by wider Cold War policy concerns, frequent crises in the Caribbean, Southeast Asia, and Berlin, but, above all by tragedy. Bulgaria and Romania had signaled their willingness for better relations with the United States. Both wanted to spur their industrialization, and Kennedy's policies to promote development seemed worth exploring. The invasion of the Bay of Pigs heightened Cold War tensions; it disrupted coordination with allies and delayed progress behind the "Iron Curtain".[43] Demonstrations took place outside U.S. embassies in the Balkans as well as in the rest of Eastern Europe. The newly reestablished mission in Sofia was ransacked and calls for protection were ignored by the Bulgarian authorities.[44] The subsequent crises over Berlin in 1961 and the Cuban Missile Crisis (CMC) in 1962 kept tensions high, fomenting changes behind the "Iron Curtain" that had a negative effect on the security situation in the Balkan peninsula and reigniting suspicions between Bulgaria and Greece. Albania would finally achieve the isolation it craved by seeking the patronage of China, while Romania would use the CMC to improve relations with the United States.[45] At loggerheads over Cyprus, Graeco-Turkish tensions combined with "flexible response," talk of an "opening to the left," and domestic political and economic pressures. Both felt that their national interests were not being valued adequately by their allies at a time of Bulgarian bellicosity and Soviet threats. The CMC affected Yugoslavia deeply too. Washington had hurt Yugoslavia's economy and its ability to access defense materiel because of its trade with Cuba. Adding insult to injury, the Americans kept Yugoslavia on the list of "captive nations." All this happened at the critical moment when Tito was staking his claim to the leadership of the Non-Aligned Movement (NAM) and worsening East–West relations could diminish the scope for the NAM to succeed. Tito denounced American actions and used delaying tactics in negotiations with them over trade and technical assistance.[46] His visit to

---

[42] National Security Action Memoranda [NSAM]: NSAM 13, re: Exchange of Persons Behind The Iron Curtain, 8 February to 14 July 1961, Papers of John F. Kennedy, Presidential Papers, National Security Files, Meetings and Memoranda, JFKNSF-328-014, John F. Kennedy Presidential Library and Museum (JFKL), Boston.

[43] John F. Kennedy, Inaugural Address Online by Gerhard Peters and John T. Woolley, *The American Presidency Project* <https://www.presidency.ucsb.edu/node/234470> (1 June 2021).

[44] Veselina Uzunova, "Bulgaria and the United States in the 60s: From Confrontation to Détente: A Cold War Case Study," *Hiperboreea: Journal of History* 6 (2019) 2: 51–58.

[45] Larry Watts, "Romania Security Policy and the Cuban Missile Crisis," Wilson Center, CWIHP e-Dossier No. 38 <https://www.wilsoncenter.org/publication/romania-security-policy-and-the-cuban-missile-crisis> (3 August 2021).

[46] *FRUS 1961–1963*, Volume XVI, *Eastern Europe; Cyprus; Greece; Turkey* (Washington: United States Government Printing Office, 1994), document 88.

the White House in October 1963 left him underwhelmed when he was met with congressional hostility and street protests.[47]

There were reservations over the value of differentiation within the Kennedy administration that led it to adopt an aloof attitude to promoting trade with the Soviet bloc and especially the Balkan countries. Its reluctance was dictated both by domestic and foreign policy concerns. Conservative groups had grown stronger and were demanding a bolder policy towards Eastern European countries.[48] By September 1963, Kennedy's foreign policy team was interpreting the Sino-Soviet split as offering confirmation that the CMC had promoted bloc fragmentation and that in mitigation the Soviets were creating "controlled instability" by piling up the pressure on areas of vulnerability such as Southeast Asia and Berlin, as well as Greece and Austria, which shared borders with the Balkans.[49] They were convinced that Soviet naval strategy with its focus on submarine construction was designed to disrupt the defense of Western Europe.[50] A de-aligned China did not offer much solace either. It needed to be factored into policy anew. Wary of antagonizing Congress, Kennedy did not dare make any moves to open China up – even along the lines of a traditional "Open Door" policy.[51]

Evaluating the utility of détente proved difficult and contentious. All could see that the Chairman of the Policy Planning Council, Walt Whitman Rostow, had a point when he stated that "détente for all its subtleties and difficulties was essentially more wholesome an environment than the eyeball-to-eyeball world of 1961–62,"[52] but he also pointed out potential disadvantages. The Allies and Third World countries could infer that through détente the superpowers might stifle their own aims and such an impression could lead to regionalism. A relaxation of tensions could also reduce "fear of communism," make "local communism respectable," and have an insidious effect, for example "on Italian and Greek domestic politics."[53] Therefore, "the art of playing the diffusion of power within the Communist world"[54] needed to be pursued with caution and only after co-

---

47 Ibid.
48 A. Paul Kubricht, "Politics and Foreign Policy".
49 *FRUS* 1961–1963, Volume VIII, *National Security Policy* (Washington: United States Government Printing Office, 1996), documents 143 and 93.
50 Ibid., document 120.
51 Ambassador James W. S. Spain, interviewed by Charles Stuart Kennedy, 31 October 1995, The Association for Diplomatic Studies and Training Foreign Affairs Oral History Project <https://www.adst.org/OH%20TOCs/Spain,%20James%20W.S.toc.pdf> (1 July 2021).
52 *FRUS* 1961–1963, VIII, document 143.
53 Ibid., document 142.
54 Ibid., document 143.

ordinating with the Western European allies[55] and informing public opinion.[56] Between September and November 1963, however, when fate tragically intervened, neither differentiation nor the Balkans received much attention because of the deteriorating situation in Vietnam.

VI. "Building Bridges"

President Lyndon Baines Johnson had to satisfy a plethora of challenging and emotionally charged popular expectations. He had to fulfill the hopes raised by his charismatic slain predecessor and those raised by his own political agenda, against a background of domestic volatility fuelled by the escalating conflict in Vietnam. His ambitious "great society" domestic program was accompanied by the equally ambitious policy of "building bridges" with Eastern Europe, his own version of differentiation. Walt Rostow designed the theoretical underpinnings of policy and would oversee its implementation as Johnson's national security advisor. "Trade" and "culture" were to be deployed to underpin national security, promote a settlement in Central Europe that would reconcile German unity with European security, and also ease the pressure in Vietnam.[57] At the core of Johnson's deployment of differentiation was always Vietnam. Romania and Yugoslavia would be singled out for special attention because of their potential to act as "back channels," in the case of the former to establish communication with Vietnam and China, and the latter to temper anti-Americanism in the NAM. It was an ambitious and risky venture seeking to generate political change in Eastern Europe by using "trade to drive hard, realistic political bargains."[58]

The policy rested on the hypothesis that in the Eastern bloc, "the current trend to autonomy" would continue. It sought to weaken the Soviet Union's grip over its satellites by taking advantage of nationalism and vanity behind the "Iron Curtain."[59] The CIA warned there was a possibility of Soviet overreaction and

---

55 NSAM 13, re: Exchange of Persons Behind The Iron Curtain, 8 February to 14 July 1961, Papers of John F. Kennedy, Presidential Papers, National Security Files, Meetings and Memoranda, JFKNSF-328-014, JFKL, Boston.
56 *FRUS* 1961–1963, VIII, document 143.
57 *FRUS* 1964–1968, Volume X, *National Security Policy* (Washington: United States Government Printing Office, 2001), document 80.
58 Thomas A. Schwartz, *Lyndon Johnson and Europe: In the Shadow of Vietnam* (Cambridge: Harvard University Press, 2003), 20; Mitchell Lerner, "'Trying to Find the Guy Who Invited Them': Lyndon Johnson, Bridge Building, and the End of the Prague Spring," *Diplomatic History* 32 (2008) 1: 77–103.
59 *FRUS* 1964–1968, X, document 84.

advised against "dramatic and flamboyant actions."[60] "Building bridges" established a loose hierarchy of eligibility. Yugoslavia remained the firm favorite, Romania was deemed worth exploring, and Bulgaria, although assigned the role of the "outsider," would not be neglected either. For "building bridges" to work, Johnson needed to review both the restrictive legislative framework on trading with Communist countries as well as his chances of success. The Miller Committee that evaluated the policy reported back in May 1965 in support of the idea and urged Johnson to promote enabling draft legislation.[61]

Securing a positive change in East–West relations was a high priority for Johnson but not in his gift. The Soviet Union, Congress and America's allies also had their roles to play. In the unstable international environment of the 1960s, the policy encouraged paranoia in both foes and allies. Vietnam diverted attention away from the procedural details for an East–West trade bill. On 11 May 1966, it was not Johnson but an unenthusiastic Rusk who sent the draft bill to a Congress becoming progressively more restive over Vietnam.[62] For such a deal to pass, it really needed Johnson, the operator, to throw his weight about. He decided, however, to take Rusk's advice and not spend too much political capital on the bill, and this sealed its fate.[63] As Post Master General John A. Gronouski put it: "The East-West Trade Bill died a-borning, [...]. It was introduced and that was all."[64] Congress hampered Johnson's policy for two years, so he moved through the powers vested in the presidency to reduce export restrictions on some U.S. goods, lifting many travel restrictions and promoting scientific and academic exchange. Both Romania and Bulgaria hungered after MFN status as they chased accelerated development and their leaders' international prominence.[65] They capitalized on any scope for maneuver within the confines of the Warsaw Pact with minimal risk, since the U.S.S.R. was encouraging its satellites to enhance trading relations with the West in order reinvigorate its own stagnating economy and gain access to new technology.[66]

---

60 *FRUS 1964–1968*, Volume XVII, *Eastern Europe* (Washington: United States Government Printing Office, 1996), document 6.
61 *FRUS 1964–1968*, Volume IX, *International Development and Economic Defense Policy*; *Commodities* (Washington: United States Government Printing Office, 1997), document 172.
62 *FRUS 1964–1968*, XVII, document 6; Editorial Note, *FRUS 1964–1968*, IX, document 181.
63 Ibid., document 172.
64 John A. Gronouski, Interview 3 (III), interviewed by Paige E. Mulhollan, 14 February 1969, oral history transcript, Lyndon B. Johnson Library Oral Histories [NAID 24617781] <https://www.discoverlbj.org/item/oh-gronouskij-19690214-3-00-04> (5 July 2021).
65 Thomas A. Schwartz, "Moving Beyond the Cold War: the Johnson Administration, Bridge-Building, and Détente," in *Beyond the Cold War: Lyndon Johnson and the New Global Challenges of the 1960s*, edited by Mark Lawrence and Frank Gavin (Oxford: Oxford University Press, 2014), 76–94.
66 Steven J. Rosen and James R. Kurth (eds.), *Theories of Economic Imperialism* (Lexington: Lexington Books, 1978), 231–60.

"Building bridges" in the Balkan peninsula was beset by obstacles. Yugoslavia needed financial assistance and American–Yugoslav relations needed attention. By 1965, the outlook for the Yugoslav economy had worsened significantly and Tito embarked on economic reforms designed to underpin Yugoslavia's faltering experiment of reconciling socialism with market economics. He needed more investment. The Johnson administration sought to improve trade with the country, assuming, wishfully, that this would give it extra leverage over Tito, compelling him to tone down his criticism of American policy in Vietnam and influence other NAM countries to do so too. The path to improved relations and sales of defense materiel proved thorny, as Congressional hostility to Tito remained high.[67]

There was also ambivalence on Tito's part. He needed to maintain equidistance from both superpowers in order to preserve his influence within the NAM. His stance over Vietnam and curtailment of diplomatic relations with Israel after the Six Days War gave him the opportunity to project an image of independence and offer support to a NAM fellow member state, Egypt, but also to appease Brezhnev. To keep the bilateral relationship with the United States ticking along, he habitually accompanied his waywardness with some pro-U.S. utterances.[68] Still, Yugoslavia had already secured a relatively advantageous position vis-à-vis its communist neighbors. It had access to normal commercial credits, PL-480 credits, and it had been awarded MFN status.[69] It was the only country Johnson could use to demonstrate that differentiation could also bring about internal liberalization. Since 1959, the Yugoslav criminal justice system had undergone some reform. In July 1966, the purging of Aleksandar Rankovic, the powerful proponent of "Yugoslavism," paved the way for further liberalization. Cosmetic exercise or not, the feeling in DC was that state control over life was loosening in Yugoslavia and that "building bridges" was working.[70]

Bucharest did not take sides in the Sino-Soviet split, but it grabbed all the opportunities it offered to distance Romania from "Soviet hegemonism."[71] Gheorghe Dej's so-called "Romanian declaration of independence" in April 1964,

---

67 *The New York Times*, 1 August 1965; David L. Larson, *United States Foreign Policy Towards Yugoslavia, 1943–1963* (Washington, D.C.: University Press of America, 1979).
68 *FRUS 1964–1968*, XVII, document 178; Jonathan Colman, *The Foreign Policy of Lyndon B. Johnson: The United States and the World, 1963–1969* (Edinburgh: University of Edinburgh Press, 2010), 116–18.
69 *FRUS 1961–1963*, XVI, document 88.
70 Dejan Djokic (ed.), *Yugoslavism: Histories of a Failed Idea, 1918–1992* (Madison: University of Wisconsin Press, 2003).
71 Elena Dragomir, "The perceived threat of hegemonism in Romania during the second détente," *Cold War History*, 12 (2012) 1: 111–34; Cezar Stanciu, "Fragile Equilibrium: Romania and the Vietnam War in the Context of the Sino-Soviet Split, 1966," *Journal of Cold War Studies* 18 (2016) 1: 161–87.

allied to his policy of "food-for-machines trade with the West," his decision to stop jamming the VoA and RFE in 1963, and the suggestion that Romania could act as a "back-channel" for the United States with North Vietnam, made Romania a good prospect for the "building bridges" program.[72] Dej's successes became clear later, during Nicolae Ceaușescu's reign of terror. Within three months of Ceaușescu's accession to power, an agreement was signed with the United States, on 1 June 1964, to establish full embassies, expand trade, and enhance cultural and scientific cooperation.[73] The Romanian shopping list impressed the United States. It ranged from machinery to technology to enhance their oil industry. The Pentagon and the Departments of the Interior and Commerce recommended that the government refuse because Romania supplied twenty per cent of North Vietnam's petroleum needs. The State Department closed ranks with the White House, even suggesting that Romania was moving towards internal liberalization.[74] Romania was also useful in approaching China. The Johnson administration used the visit of the Romanian premier, Ion Gheorghe Maurer, to convey to China that the United States had "no designs on her territory or her philosophy" and that it wished to trade.[75] Ceaușescu also proved to be more reliable than Tito, as he was not encumbered by connections to the NAM.[76] Despite furious congressional opposition, Johnson's funneling of investment to Romania would increase.[77]

Elitza Stanoeva has pointed out the 1960s were "a particularly dynamic period in Bulgaria's interactions with the West."[78] The Council of Mutual Economic Assistance (CMEA) was a rudder of stability for the Bulgarian economy, but Bulgaria coveted brisker industrialization. Post-Stalinist economic reforms of-

---

72 *FRUS* 1964–1968, XVII, document 141.
73 Ibid., document 143.
74 Ibid., document 150.
75 Ibid., document 157.
76 The CIA's Freedom of Information Act Electronic Reading Room <https://www.cia.gov/readingroom/docs/DOC_0000095039.pdf> (1 April 2021); James G. Hershberg, "The Soviet Bloc and the Aftermath of the June 1967 War," CWIHP e-Dossier No.13 <https://www.wilsoncenter.org/publication/the-soviet-bloc-and-the-aftermath-the-june-1967-war> (15 April 2021); "Polish Record of Meeting of Soviet-bloc leaders (and Tito) in Budapest (excerpts)," 11 July 1967, Wilson Centre, History and Public Policy Program Digital Archive, KC PZPR, XI A/13, AAN, document obtained by James G. Hershberg and Wanda Jarzabek; translated by Jan Chowaniec <https://digitalarchive.wilsoncenter.org/document/113622> (3 August 2021).
77 *FRUS* 1964–1968, Volume XIV, *Soviet Union* (Washington: United States Government Printing Office, 2001), document 156.
78 Elitza Stanoeva, "Balancing Between Socialist Internationalism and Economic Internationalisation: Bulgaria's economic contacts with the EEC," in *European Socialist Regimes' Fateful Engagement with the West: National Strategies in the Long 1970s*, edited by Angela Romano and Federico Romero (London: Routledge, 2020), 161–89.

fered the Bulgarians the opportunity to explore trade with the West vigorously.[79] In 1962, Todor Zhivkov became prime minister. His approach to accessing the glitter of "building bridges" and trade with the EEC was to dip his toe in the water carefully so as to not upset relations with the Soviet Union. Relations with the United States remained difficult with "spontaneous" demonstrations besieging the U.S. embassy in Sofia with alarming regularity, prompting an American diplomat to comment that improvement in relations between the two countries was like "the first smiles one gets from a [...] baby. One is not entirely sure whether the smile is real or simply a gas pain."[80] Yet, persistently, Zhivkov and his foreign minister Ivan Bashev conveyed messages to the United States that they wished to expand scientific, technological, industrial, and cultural exchanges, and buy entire industrial plants, even if all this meant "financial sacrifice" for Bulgaria. What Bulgaria wanted above all else was MFN status.[81] The U.S. embassy was particularly supportive. It informed DC that Bulgaria would not move away from the Soviet Union because of its economic and cultural affinity, but in terms of internal liberalization, Bulgaria was "among the moderately progressive regimes of Eastern Europe."[82] Washington, however, could not overlook that Bulgaria was a country that was exporting weapons, know-how, and aid to anti-Western forces in Africa and Latin America.[83]

"Building bridges" precipitated unexpected consequences in Eastern Europe and the Balkans. Bulgaria, Romania, and Yugoslavia sought increased engagement, expanded trade, and cultural and scientific exchanges but liberalization, however, remained moot. At the same time, it caused resentment and unease in America's allies in the region. It fused with other sources of instability that agitated the countries of NATO's Southern Flank, namely the aftereffects from the CMC, strains over Cyprus, disquiet over the possibility of a relaxation of tensions between East and West, and moves towards more inclusive socio-political systems. Feelings that trust was being compromised arose in Greece and

---

79 Ivan T. Berend, "What is Central and Eastern Europe?", *European Journal of Social Theory* 8 (2005) 4: 401–16.
80 *FRUS* 1964–1968, XVII, document 32.
81 Ibid., documents 34, 35.
82 Ibid., document 32.
83 Radoslav Yordanov, "Fishing in the desert: Unravelling the Soviet Bloc's economic activities and intelligence gathering in Ethiopia in the 1960s, with particular reference to Bulgaria," *The International History Review* 43 (2021) 1: 109–21; Jordan Baev, "Bulgarian Military and Humanitarian Aid to Third World Countries: 1955–75," in *Warsaw Pact intervention in the Third World: Aid and Influence in the Cold War*, edited by Philip Muehlenbeck and Natalia Telepneva (London: I.B. Tauris, 2018), 298–326; "Information on Latin America and Cuba: Delivery of Weapons to Cuba and Latin America," 2 February 1966, Wilson Centre, History and Public Policy Program Digital Archive, International History Declassified, Central State Archive of Bulgaria (TsDA), Sofia, Fond 1-B, Opis 51, a.e. 592, edited by Jordan Baev <https://digitalarchive.wilsoncenter.org/document/116372> (3 August 2021).

Turkey. The tensions proved too much for the fragile Greek democracy to endure and a junta of erratic and opportunistic army colonels hijacked it in April 1967. Turkey continued its road to political and social instability, seemingly never being able to come to terms with the "Johnson Letter" of 1964. Both countries remained in NATO, but keeping them on board would soon pose challenges to NATO's cohesion.

By 1968, Soviet and some Eastern European leaders came to perceive "building bridges" as malicious both for them and for communism per se.[84] Vlad Zubok, in a deeply evocative essay, has painted a picture of a Soviet leadership that was divided over de-Stalinization and how to deal with moves towards more autonomy in its European satellites while it faced a Russian society also split over how far to embrace the spirit of the 1960s.[85] The Soviet Union decided it had had enough of both the *zeitgeist* and differentiation and confronted its dilemmas by asserting its authority, adopting the "Brezhnev Doctrine", and indicating forcefully that any "bridge" ought to be built directly with it and not over it. Czechoslovakia's fate in August 1968 would put an abrupt end to "building bridges" at a moment when Johnson had come to see it as the cornerstone of his legacy. Its brutal demise, however, should not obscure the fact that despite the challenges it faced, its contradictions and half-hearted application, it had not been futile. As Thomas Schwartz has pointed out, "Johnson's achievements [. . .] stand out as creating the essential basis for easing relations."[86] The legacy of "building bridges" in the Balkans was, however, more problematic. It reinforced existing suspicions and resentments.[87]

VII. Superpower Détente and Differentiation

In 1967, in his Bohemian Club Speech, Richard M. Nixon elaborated on his thinking on foreign policy. Under his stewardship, the United States would encourage "more trade with the USSR and Eastern Europe," and taking aim at Johnson's foreign policy, he continued, "I believe in building bridges but we should build only our end of the bridge."[88] Nixon and his national security

---

84 Mitchell Lerner, "'Trying to Find the Guy Who Invited Them': Lyndon Johnson, Bridge Building, and the End of the Prague Spring," *Diplomatic History* 32 (2008) 1: 77–103.
85 Vladislav Zubok, "Soviet society in the 1960s," in *The Prague Spring and the Warsaw Pact Invasion of Czechoslovakia in 1968*, edited by Günter Bischof et al. (Lanham: Lexington Books, 2010), 75–102.
86 Schwartz, "Lyndon Johnson and Europe," 20.
87 Pedaliu, "The US, the Balkans and Détente," 197–218.
88 *FRUS 1969–1976*, Volume I, *Foundations of Foreign Policy, 1969–1972* (Washington, DC.: United States Government Printing Office, 2003), document 2.

advisor Henry Kissinger confronted power shifts in the international system by seeking a direct understanding with the U.S.S.R. through negotiations, trade, and arms control. On the surface, it seemed to use the same tools as all its predecessors, but superpower détente would be a tenuous policy of deliberate ambiguity, and a "sticking plaster" strategy to enable the United States to overcome the international and domestic price Vietnam was exacting. Nixon and Kissinger tried to pursue differentiation and détente simultaneously and balance out clashing, almost incompatible outcomes, as differentiation aimed to foment change by compromising the foundations of the Soviet domination of Eastern Europe, and détente to reestablish the primacy of the superpowers. This was a détente with no agreed rules – one where relations with the U.S.S.R. would be prioritized over relations with Eastern European states while volatile areas such as the Mediterranean were excluded.[89] Selective differentiation and détente increased Balkan vulnerability and local countries came to perceive the "era of negotiations" as a high-risk, zero-sum game for the region.[90]

Most Balkan states had invested in a continuing "High Cold War" as assuring their security, development, political stability, and social cohesion. Bulgaria, Greece, Romania, and Turkey saw any kind of détente as an unwelcome development. Yugoslavia had been less than comfortable with the casual way many NAM leaders treated Soviet actions in Czechoslovakia.[91] Now, it needed détente for the NAM to continue to be relevant and to prosper but the aloofness of superpower détente affected it intensely. Its interests in the Mediterranean and the Balkans did not align with those of the United States.[92] Tito, during his first full state visit to DC in 1971, was told by President Nixon that countries could "have good relations with the United States but without going so far as to provoke the Soviets into using their might to stop movement toward independence."[93] Nixon's caveats came at a time when Yugoslavia was negotiating to resolve complex internal, international, and economic problems and Brezhnev was toying with the idea of using its economic problems and its nationalities, stirring for greater autonomy, to make good Zhivkov's threat "to introduce order in Yugoslavia, too."[94]

---

89 Effie G. H. Pedaliu, "'A Sea of Confusion': The Mediterranean and Détente, 1969–1974," *Diplomatic History* 33 (2009) 4: 735–50.
90 Pedaliu, "The US, the Balkans and Détente, 1963–73," 203–8.
91 John R. Lampe, "Yugoslavia's Foreign Policy in Balkan Perspective: Tracking between the Superpowers and Non-Alignment," *East Central Europe* 40 (2013) 1–2: 97–113.
92 Alvin Z. Rubinstein, "The Evolution of Yugoslavia's Mediterranean Policy," *International Journal* 27 (1972) 4: 528–45.
93 *FRUS* 1969–1976, Volume XXIX, *Eastern Europe; Eastern Mediterranean, 1969–1972* (Washington: United States Government Printing Office, 2007), document 234.
94 Milorad Lazić, "The Soviet Intervention that Never Happened: Records of a Tito-Brezhnev call suggest the Kremlin mulled intervention in Yugoslavia in 1971" in *Sources and Methods*

Figure 1: President Nixon and President Tito during formal welcoming ceremonies on the White House lawn in 1971. (Source: Bettmann / Getty Images)

For Nixon and Kissinger, Romania was a better indicator of the Soviet mood towards détente and differentiation. They focused differentiation on it to the detriment of Yugoslavia, thus clearing the path for Ceaușescu to emerge as America's "favorite dictator." Romania considered détente as having the potential to bring about a squeeze of the small powers by the superpowers, and asserted its right to trade directly with the EEC and the United States.[95] For Bulgaria, détente coincided with a moment when exporting to the EEC was becoming more difficult.[96] Finally, Greece and Turkey had their own misgivings. The Greek Junta perceived that with détente, its geostrategic importance would be diminished. For the Turks, talk of détente was increasing domestic instability and also opening up the prospect of reduced financial aid reaching Ankara. Balkan states on both sides of the ideological divide were coming to the conclusion that the superpowers were promoting their own interests and relegating

---

(A blog and the History and Public Policy Program, Wilson Center), 4 December 2017 <https://www.wilsoncenter.org/blog-post/the-soviet-intervention-never-happened> (2 July 2021).

95 Dragomir, "The Perceived Threat of Hegemonism," 124; Angela Romano, "Untying Cold War Knots: The EEC and Eastern Europe in the Long 1970s," *Cold War History* 14 (2014) 2: 164–5.

96 Stanoeva, "Balancing Between Socialist Internationalism and Economic Internationalisation," 161–89.

theirs, and that détente was agitating their domestic politics in an unwholesome way.[97]

Superpower détente, as pursued by Nixon, raised real fears in the region of a "Melian" fate and bred regionalism, encouraging dialogue among Balkan states across the Cold War divide.[98] The Greek dictators wished to show their Western allies that contempt for their "regime" did not prevent them from seeking out other allies. They weaponized relations with their Balkan neighbors and the Soviet Union in their efforts to blackmail the West. Romania, in turn, felt uncomfortable with Soviet and American hegemonic tendencies and superpower détente exacerbated its fears.[99] Ceaușescu pursued the cause of multilateral détente as a means of undermining the Soviet grip over the communist states of the Balkans.[100] The Bulgarians pushed back against such actions vehemently, since their wish to accelerate improvements in relations with their neighbors was not accompanied by any desire to undermine their close relationship with Moscow. In 1968, while airing his misgivings about transmitters for VoA and RFE programs on Greek soil, the Bulgarian Ambassador to the United States, Luben Guerassimov, had also told Assistant Secretary John M. Leddy that the dictatorship in Greece "was hindering the development of a better atmosphere in the Balkans."[101] But soon Bulgaria would liaise directly with the Greek dictators. By May 1970, Bashev held his nose and visited Athens. There was no mention of political prisoners in Greece but a series of agreements were struck. In autumn, Gogo Kozma, the Albania foreign minister visited Sofia, Zhivkov met Ceaușescu and progress was made in defusing tensions in Yugoslav–Bulgarian relations that had been evident since January 1969 over "the Macedonian issue." Bemused by all this activity, Suleiman Demirel, the Turkish prime minister, also visited Sofia. In June 1971, the Romanian foreign minister, Corneliu Mănescu, visited Athens to promote Ceaușescu's plans for Balkan cooperation.[102] The regional détente was strictly bilateral in nature, but the maneuvering coincided with Chinese diplomatic and commercial activities in the Balkans. Soviet concerns arose that the United States, after its opening to China, was using it to undermine Moscow's

---

97 *FRUS* 1961–1963, VIII, document 142.
98 Ivor F. Porter (UK delegation to NATO) to Bryan Sparrow (EESD, FCO), 12 February 1971, TNA/FCO 28/1501; Pedaliu, "The US, the Balkans and Détente, 1963–73," 207.
99 Paschalis Pechlivanis, "An Uneasy Triangle: Nicolae Ceaușescu, the Greek Colonels and the Greek Communists (1967–1974)," *International History Review*, 43 (2021) 3: 598–613; Ioannis D. Stefanidis, "America's Projection and Promotion of Democracy: The Voice of America, the Greek Dictatorship and Ceausescu's Romania," *Modern Greek Studies Yearbook* 32 (2017) 33: 167–237.
100 Cezar Stanciu, "A lost chance for Balkan cooperation? The Romanian view on 'regional micro-détente', 1969–75," *Cold War History* 19 (2019) 3: 421–39.
101 *FRUS* 1964–1968, XVII, document 35.
102 Pechlivanis, "An Uneasy Triangle," 598–613.

position in the peninsula. Such complications led the United States to consider the exploratory Balkan micro-détente as a hindrance to its wider interests.[103] In this environment, differentiation could not be deployed fully without undermining détente. The strategy of "linkage" that Nixon/Kissinger pursued towards the U.S.S.R. entailed compromise and accepting, tacitly, Soviet primacy in Eastern Europe in return for concessions in Vietnam.[104]

The exploratory Balkan micro-détente did not have the vigor to survive a world oil crisis in 1973, or the onset of the slow death of superpower détente when its overhyped aims encountered the Yom Kippur War, political upheaval in Italy, and the Turkish invasion of Cyprus. These events combined to reveal the limitations of superpower détente as a process, its haphazard arrangements, and its crude treatment of volatile areas such as the Mediterranean and the Middle East.[105] As the philosopher and poet George Santayana put it, "wisdom comes by disillusionment." Kissinger was "neuralgic" about the Mediterranean, but he could not "read" it or appraise with a cool head the collapse of the dictatorships in the Southern Flank. He saw only "nightmares and not opportunities." His instincts proved wrong on Portugal and Greece and then, later, Spain.[106] The realization was dawning that "neither SALT nor trade nor credits had basically altered the competitive character of the East–West relationship."[107] Détente and differentiation intersected with the dynamics unleashed by *Ostpolitik* and the EEC's growth as a political and economic actor.[108] For the Balkans, opportunity and security seemed to point firmly to Brussels and Helsinki. The Helsinki spirit offered scope for greater maneuver between the superpowers, but access to the EEC could flourish only if tensions between the latter were kept low. The Balkan states revised their dim view of détente and would resist its demise later.

President Gerald R. Ford had to ensure the survival of the increasingly unpopular policy of détente in domestic public opinion at a time when his European allies were pursuing a version based on more liberal aspirations. At the same

---

103 Pedaliu, "The US, the Balkans and Détente," 197–218.
104 Douglas E. Selvage, "Transforming the Soviet Sphere of Influence? U.S.-Soviet Détente and Eastern Europe, 1969–1976," *Diplomatic History* 33 (2009) 4: 671–87.
105 Pedaliu, "A Sea of Confusion," 735–50.
106 Victor Gavin, "The Nixon and Ford Administrations and the Future of Post-Franco Spain (1970–6)," *International History Review* 38 (2016) 5: 930–42; Mario del Pero, "The Cold War and the Portuguese Revolution," and Charles Powell, "International Dimensions of Democratisation: Revisiting the Spanish Case," in *The Greek Junta and the International System: A Case Study of Southern European Dictatorships, 1967–74*, edited by Antonis Klapsis et al. (London: Routledge, 2020), 203–14 and 215–27; Thomas A. Schwartz, *Henry Kissinger and American Power* (New York: Hill and Wang, 2020).
107 *FRUS 1977–1980*, Volume I, *Foundations of Foreign Policy* (Washington: United States Government Printing Office, 2014), document 66.
108 Suvi Kansikas, *Socialist Countries Face the European Community: Soviet-Bloc Controversies over East-West Trade* (New York: Peter Lang, 2014).

time, Ford needed to contain the damage done to U.S. prestige by Vietnam, Watergate, his predecessor's uncritical support of Southern European dictators, and possible conflict between Greece and Turkey. In the background, the U.S.S.R. was determined to capitalize on American woes worldwide. Kissinger's retention at the helm of the State Department ensured the continuity of Nixonian foreign policy in both spirit and substance at a moment when both the United States and the world were changing fast.[109] Ford needed to decide how to apply differentiation to the Balkans when the region had entered a period of intense instability and insecurity. The Balkans were coming to terms with sluggish growth, growing deficits, rising inflation, the consequences of local conflict, and the return to democracy in Southern Europe. There were internal tremors in Yugoslavia first and then in Bulgaria and Albania as secularism gave way to growing identity politics, separatism, and a more assertive Islam.[110] All propelled another bout of Balkan cooperation for security, economic development, and local solutions across bloc allegiances. The Balkan détente of the second half of the 1970s was different in nature than its earlier iteration. It was about creating enough space for national interests to be pursued even when the superpowers preferred to ignore them.

It was initiated by democratic Greece, which decided that its best defense lay in the internationalization of its problems by rallying friends, searching for new economic and trade relations with old foes, and seeking entry to the EEC. As Eirini Karamouzi and Lykourgos Kourkouvelas have discussed in their respective articles, Constantinos Karamanlis, the Greek prime minister, took "the Helsinki spirit" on the road, visiting Belgrade, Bucharest, and Sofia and attempting to rekindle the earlier, now moribund, Balkan détente.[111] He adopted an inclusive approach. His *Nordpolitik* was not devoid of elements of *Ostpolitik*; Turkey was not excluded.[112] Balkan détente offered the Karamanlis government breathing space to reprioritize Greek defense away from the "danger from the North," now deemed to be less imminent, and address its vulnerability to a NATO ally, Turkey, but without forgetting that it faced a double and concurrent threat from both its

---

109 *FRUS* 1969–1976, Volume XXXVIII, Part 1, *Foundations of Foreign Policy, 1973–1976* (Washington: United States Government Printing Office, 2012), document 38.
110 Fikret Karcic, "Islamic Revival in the Balkans 1970–1992," *Islamic Studies* 36 (1997) 2–3: 565– 81.
111 Eirini Karamouzi, "Managing the 'Helsinki Spirit' in the Balkans: The Greek Initiative for Balkan Co-operation, 1975–1976," *Diplomacy & Statecraft* 24 (2013) 4: 597–618; Lykourgos Kourkouvelas, "Détente as a Strategy: Greece and the Communist World, 1974–9," *International History Review* 35 (2013) 5: 1052–67.
112 *FRUS* 1977–1980, Volume XXI, *Cyprus; Turkey; Greece* (Washington: United States Government Printing Office, 2014), document 184.

neighbor and communism.[113] John Foster Dulles' "hooked fish" was not about to snap the line no matter how disappointed it became with the Americans' mealymouthed approach towards the Turkish threat. Greece's temporary withdrawal from the integrated military command of NATO reflected this, but it was not a departure. Karamanlis never sought to hinder the operation of the U.S. bases in the country despite the huge political cost to his own party.[114] "Greece belong[ed] to the West,"[115] but it would also adopt regionalism and multilateralism, the most available diplomatic weapons to the small powers.[116]

Bulgaria joined in but rejected any multilateral Balkan approaches that could antagonize the Soviets. It kept Moscow informed of local diplomatic initiatives while making it clear that it did not to wish to become a mere onlooker and pointing out to Leonid Brezhnev that Bulgaria's isolation would also be detrimental to Soviet regional interests.[117] Zhivkov, fearing that "the Cypriot scenario" could be reenacted against his country and under pressure from the Soviet Union, was relieved when the Turks sought improvement in their bilateral relationship, and he reciprocated. Turkey and Bulgaria signed an Agreement of Good-Neighborliness and Cooperation in 1975, and a new trade agreement in 1976.[118] Expanded trade and cultural diplomacy were the tools Bulgaria chose for international engagement[119] and Zhivkov's attitude to Balkan cooperation mirrored his priorities. He was willing to act as the Soviet Union's *locum tenens* for as long as his interests coincided with Soviet aims, which was the case most of the time.[120]

---

113 Effie G. H. Pedaliu, "'Footnotes' as an Expression of Distrust? The United States and the NATO 'Flanks' in the Last Two Decades of the Cold War," in *Trust, but Verify: The Politics of Uncertainty and the Transformation of the Cold War Order, 1969-1991*, edited by Martin Klimke et al. (Stanford: Stanford University Press, 2016), 237–58.
114 FRUS 1977-1980, XXI, document 21.
115 Eirini Karamouzi, *Greece, the EEC and the Cold War 1974-1979* (London: Palgrave Macmillan, 2014).
116 Angela Romano and Laurien Crump, "Challenging the superpower straitjacket (1965-1975): Multilateralism as an instrument of smaller powers," in *Margins for Manoeuvre: The Influence of Smaller Powers on the Cold War Era*, edited by Laurien Crump and Susanna Erlandsson (New York: Routledge, 2021): 13–31.
117 Kostadin Grozev and Jordan Baev, "Bulgaria, Balkan Diplomacy, and the Road to Helsinki," in *Helsinki 1975 and the Transformation of Europe*, edited by Oliver Bange and Gottfried Niedhart (New York: Berghahn Books, 2008), 160–74.
118 Feroz Ahmad, *The Turkish Experiment in Democracy, 1950-1975* (Boulder: Westview, 1977), 407–9; Michael B. Bishku, "Turkish-Bulgarian Relations: From Conflict and Distrust to Cooperation over Minority Issues and International Politics," *Mediterranean Quarterly* 14 (2003) 2: 77–94.
119 Theodora Dragostinova, "The East in the West: Bulgarian Culture in the United States of America during the Global 1970s," *Journal of Contemporary History* 53 (2018) 1: 212–39.
120 FRUS 1977-1980, Volume XX, *Eastern Europe* (Washington: United States Government Printing Office, 2015), document 90.

Romania saw this as another chance to promote its persistent search for multilateral regional dialogue to undermine the blocs, gain greater access to local markets, enhance Ceaușescu's international role, and bolster his increasingly repressive rule. Ceaușescu sought to promote Romanian regional influence by acting as a bridge between China and the Balkans,[121] yet he did not scorn the opportunities bilateralism could yield. He achieved improvement in Romanian relations with Bulgaria, Greece, Turkey, and Yugoslavia. In 1975, he welcomed to Bucharest both Karamanlis and his Turkish counterpart Bülent Ecevit.[122] For Turkey, mired in socio-political and economic turmoil as well as international disapproval, renewed Balkan détente offered the means to allay the fears of its neighbors and block the unfolding Greek regional "charm offensive." It prioritized reconciliation with Bulgaria for fear that improved Graeco-Bulgarian relations could solidify into a security concern.[123] It remained loyal to NATO, despite Ecevit's threats. However, in its effort to mitigate the effects the half-hearted U.S. arms embargo over Cyprus was having on its ailing economy, rising oil prices, and the costs of occupation, it reached out to the U.S.S.R.[124]

Karamanlis' "step-by-step" rapprochement with Greece's neighbors culminated in the Athens Conference in 1976, reopening the "Balkan kaleidoscope," as Richard Clogg put it at the time.[125] All Balkan states were represented apart from Albania. They all wanted more freedom for maneuver, but apart from Romania, at this stage, no other participant wished to do away with their patrons' protection. Despite the fact that four of the participants were plagued by intractable disputes, Bulgaria and Yugoslavia over the "Macedonian issue" and Greece and Turkey over Cyprus and the Aegean Sea, all sat around the table and talked. In time, Karamanlis's rapprochement with Bulgaria, which he had started simply to blunt the "threat from the north," developed into direct personal diplomacy with Zhivkov. The two rebuilt the Graeco-Bulgarian relationship on more constructive and enduring foundations.[126] This success opened channels of communication

---

121 Pedaliu, "The US, the Balkans and Détente," 197–218.
122 Michael M. Boll, "Turkey between East and West: The Regional Alternative," *The World Today* 35 (1979) 9: 360–68.
123 Ferenc A. Váli, *Bridge across the Bosphorus: The Foreign Policy of Turkey* (Baltimore: Johns Hopkins University Press, 1971), 205; Ilhan Uzgel, "The Balkans: Turkey's Stabilizing Role," in *Turkey in World Politics: An Emerging Multiregional Power*, edited by Barry Rubin and Kemal Kirisci (Boulder: Lynne Rienner, 2001), 49–70.
124 Cissy E. G. Wallace, "Soviet Economic and Technical Cooperation with Developing Countries: the Turkish Case," unpublished PhD. thesis, LSE, 1990, 110–13; Gökay Bülent, *Soviet Eastern Policy and Turkey, 1920–1991: Soviet Foreign Policy, Turkey and Communism* (London: Routledge, 2006), 104–5.
125 Richard Clogg, "Balkan Kaleidoscope," *The World Today* 32 (1976) 8: 301–07.
126 Nikolai Todorov, *The Ambassador as Historian: An Eyewitness Account of Bulgarian Greek Relations in the 1980s* (New York: Aristide D. Caratzas, 1999); Karamouzi, "Managing the 'Helsinki Spirit' in the Balkans," 597–618; Kourkouvelas, "Détente as a Strategy," 1052–67.

and enabled anemic trust to develop, leading *Pathé News* as well as the Foreign Office to comment that it had reduced 'tension in the Balkans'.[127] It also shaped the regional environment the new U.S. administration would encounter upon President Carter's election.

VIII. The Balkans and the withering of superpower détente

In his election campaign, President Carter signposted that he understood American public opinion's growing introspection and fatigue with foreign policy adventures. Any suspicion of continuity with the Nixon–Ford–Kissinger era had to be dispelled. His promise to restore America's moral authority had proven popular, but in an increasingly interdependent world where neither superpower could fully control rising geopolitical tensions, morality and realism would clash. He had inherited an already "wounded détente" that, during his presidency, became all but "a policy of nominal but suspended détente."[128] In view of vocal transnational activism and a resurgent Congress, Carter calculated that he had to conclude the SALT II negotiations swiftly while highlighting the Soviet Union's main weaknesses and contradictions: "the mistreatment of their own citizens"[129] and an economy that could not meet their aspirations.[130]

Up until Carter, there had been some faint-hearted mention of "internal liberalization," but human rights abuses were never an obstacle to applying differentiation. Differing priorities and tactics within Carter's foreign policy team led to an inability to identify the issues where compromise with the Soviet Union could be achieved. Human rights as a weapon was wielded in a heavy-handed way by Zbigniew Brzezinski, Carter's national security advisor, undermining the more nuanced approach of the State Department, and made "the Soviets feel [...] hemmed in,"[131] reducing the United States' ability to harness the tensions generated by its human rights policy and prevent these from harming progress on

---

127 Embassy in Sofia report, 2 February 1976, TNA/FCO 28/2866; *Greece: Bulgarian President Zhivkov Meets Karamanlis 1979*, 1:20 min., Corfu, Reuters, 30 April 1979, Reuters – British Pathé – Historical Collection <https://www.britishpathe.com/video/VLVA18GIGHGDAQOA4L7S2WRANW0XK-GREECE-BULGARIAN-PRESIDENT-ZHIVKOV-MEETS-KARAMANLIS/query/Corfu> (10 May 2021).
128 Raymond Garthoff, Final Report to NSC, 22 December 1982 <https://www.cis.pitt.edu/nceer/pre1998/1982-625-4-Garthoff.pdf> (4 February 2021).
129 Stuart E. Eizenstat, *President Carter: The White House Years* (London: Macmillan/St. Martin's Publishing Group, 2018).
130 Elizabeth Clayton, "Rising Demand and Unstable Supply: The Prospects for Soviet Grain Imports," *American Journal of Agricultural Economics* 67 (1985) 5: 1044–8.
131 Zbigniew Brzezinski, *Power and Principle: Memoirs of the National Security Adviser, 1977–1981* (New York: Farrar, Straus & Giroux, 1983), 162.

SALT II.¹³² David Skidmore maintained, "the tragedy of the Carter Administration was one of historical timing."¹³³ Its policy was directed towards a Soviet Union that was increasingly adopting a bunker mentality. The "spirit of Helsinki" facilitated the growth of networks across the Cold War divide, and transformed dissent in Soviet bloc.¹³⁴ It gave dissidents behind the "Iron Curtain" hope that their anguish would not go unheard; their message chimed with international public opinion, but made the Soviet leadership more defensive and eager to reassert its control over Eastern Europe and double down on emphasizing 'national sovereignty'.¹³⁵ At the Belgrade Conference of 1977, the deterioration of relations between East and West revealed a waning of the will to approach the Cold War through a spirit of compromise.

"Historical timing" and regional dynamics posed challenges to Carter's efforts to apply differentiation to the communist Balkans states. All, irrespective of bloc allegiance, viewed the dissonance between "national sovereignty" and "human rights" with cynicism and most leaned towards national independence. The contradictions and inflexibility of Carter's and Brzezinski's differentiation influenced outcomes in a region now reconciled to détente and ready cooperate with a newly democratized Greece now distanced from NATO and seeking entry to the EEC. The Athens conference was not an inconsequential affair. It was followed in 1979 by a meeting in Ankara, in 1981 in Sofia, in 1982 in Bucharest, and in 1984 and 1988 in Belgrade, where the first foreign ministers' conference took place. Issues connected with development and growth proved the best areas for cooperation, as they had been in the past, although the strained Graeco-Turkish relationship continued to create complications.

Carter encountered this effervescent environment in the Balkans. He had two levers in his relations with the communist countries: either offering them a "big enough carrot" or using a "big enough stick." In the end, he found that he could use neither, as threatening to ditch differentiation at this juncture was deemed counterproductive. He had to pacify his allies, restore American authority in the region while curbing the U.S.S.R. from capitalizing on the woes of the Southern flank. He had to absorb more instability due to his prevarication over European defense and Tito's failing health. Carter's differentiation thus had to be accommodated within a "détente" that dared not speak its name and combined with the promotion of human rights and intensified covert operations behind the "Iron

---

132 *FRUS* 1977–1980, XX, document 17.
133 David Skidmore, *Reversing Course: Carter's Foreign Policy and the Failure of Reform* (Nashville: Vanderbilt University Press, 1996).
134 Sarah B. Snyder, *Human Rights Activism and the End of the Cold War* (New York: Cambridge University Press, 2011).
135 *FRUS* 1977–1980, XX, document 36.

Curtain."[136] Brzezinski saw covert action as the most effective means to achieve U.S. political objectives and "to produce internal evolution in the Soviet Union and Eastern Europe."[137] Investment was sought for upgraded transmitters for RFE and Radio Liberty (RL) as well as the CIA's "book program" to expand human rights activism.[138] All the while, Eastern European governments grew more sullen.

The publicizing of human rights abuses in the Eastern bloc allied with differentiation was a double-edged sword for the U.S. government. It could never deliver the unwaveringly moral policy that the public expected and the nuances of differentiation and the realities of its application came to hurt Carter personally.[139] For the purposes of differentiation, Presidential Directive 21 classified Eastern European countries, and, by extension, the Balkan countries according to their degree of internal liberalization and extent of independence from the U.S.S.R. in international affairs. Measuring internal liberalization remained problematic and such stratification did not give real scope for rewarding those that made some progress or sanctioning those that regressed. Isolationist Albania was thus left to its own devices and preferential treatment for Yugoslavia was upgraded. Romania was no longer ranked above Yugoslavia, but its eligibility to "receive preferred treatment" was reaffirmed. PD-21 placed Bulgaria on a tier that specified that "no initiatives ought to be taken to improve relations unless it tangibly and demonstrably advance[d] specific US interests."[140] Thus, PD-21 established a rigid pecking order which dispensed with experimentation – hitherto a *sine qua non* of U.S. engagement with the Balkans – and did not always work as the United States had intended.

As early as March 1977, the Carter administration decided to adhere to the recommendations of NSC-28 that "using withdrawal of MFN treatment as a sanction against human rights" was not desirable as it was deemed to set "a damaging precedent."[141] Both Yugoslavia and Romania avoided pressure and increased their demands for U.S. finance and military supplies, which included sensitive new technology and police equipment even as Ceaușescu's increasing

---

136 *FRUS* 1977–1980, XX, documents 1, 17, 20, 23, 49, 52, 54, 58, 59.
137 Ibid., document 46.
138 Ibid., documents 3, 17, 20, 23, 49, 52, 54, 58, 59.
139 Cyrus R. Vance, *Hard Choices* (New York: Simon and Schuster, 1983), 422.
140 *FRUS* 1977–1980, XX, document 16.
141 *FRUS* 1977–1980, Volume II, *Human Rights and Humanitarian Affairs* (Washington: United States Government Printing Office, 2013), document 73. For the full document see Memorandum: Human Rights, 8 July 1977, Presidential Review *Memoranda* (PRM) 28, Jimmy Carter <https://www.jimmycarterlibrary.gov/assets/documents/memorandums/prm28.pdf> (3 August 2021).

despotism and repression was becoming apparent.¹⁴² Charter 77 and the Jiu Valley miners' strike attracted yet more attention to conditions there. The U.S. Congress's ire grew and made the renewal of Romania's MFN status an uncomfortable annual ritual that necessitated a presidential waiver from "the freedom-of-emigration requirements" specified in the Jackson-Vanik amendment of 3 August 1975.¹⁴³ As Paschalis Pechlivanis puts it, "the continuity that Carter showed in his approach to Romania is indicative of his failure to efficiently implement the human rights principle in his foreign policy."¹⁴⁴ Nor could the United States meet Yugoslav and Romanian requests, as they involved supplying systems deemed to be too sensitive.¹⁴⁵ It left both dissatisfied and Carter open to charges of hypocrisy when he failed to link publicly the refusal of such requests with human rights while the international media failed to highlight his tougher stance on Bulgaria.¹⁴⁶

Relations with Bulgaria had been on a good footing since 1975, when it had signed a consular agreement with the United States. In 1977, there was a cultural exchange agreement, renewed again in 1979, in 1978 a scientific exchange agreement, and in 1979 an agricultural agreement. From 1978, Petur Mladenov, the Bulgarian foreign minister, even employed a New York public relations firm to advise on acquiring MNF status and Export-Import Bank loans. All Bulgarian efforts were rebuffed, despite the Carter administration's decision to treat it "as a sovereign state responsible for its own actions." Carter's differentiation simply could not accommodate a country unwilling to compromise its close links with the Soviet Union or its erratic behavior internationally.¹⁴⁷ Raymond Garthoff, the experienced U.S. ambassador to Bulgaria, held that Bulgaria's human rights record was no worse than Romania's or Hungary's, that were receiving preferential treatment, and that the Bulgarians appeared to be making better progress on issues of concern.¹⁴⁸ They had expedited matters swiftly in "the divided family cases" in their jurisdiction, as the case of the family of Atanas Slavov, a Bulgarian writer who resided in New York showed and they were not blocking emigration.¹⁴⁹ It was also the first Eastern European country to settle favorably the

---

142 *FRUS* 1977–1980, XX, document 252; *FRUS* 1977–1980, II, documents 206, 223, 224, 228, 231, 234.
143 Paschalis Pechlivanis, *America and Romania in the Cold War: A Differentiated Détente, 1969–80* (London: Routledge, 2019), 140–63.
144 Ibid., 179.
145 *FRUS* 1977–1980, XX, documents 246 and 252.
146 John R. Lampe, "Yugoslavia's foreign policy in Balkan perspective: Tracking between the superpowers and non-alignment," *East Central Europe* 40 (2013) 1–2: 97–113.
147 *FRUS* 1977–1980, XX, document 88.
148 Ibid., documents 91, 92, 93.
149 Theodora K. Dragostinova, *The Cold War from the Margins: A Small Socialist State on the Global Cultural Scene* (Ithaca: Cornell University Press, 2021).

claims of private American bondholders. In 1979, relations between Bulgaria and the U.S.S.R. appeared to tense over economic planning, future industrialization, and Bulgaria's sustained efforts to improve relations with the United States and the EEC.[150] Western observers speculated whether it would "take the Romanian [...] path."[151] Garthoff's suggested that this was a good moment for the United States to grant it preferential economic treatment and lessen its economic reliance on the U.S.S.R. His advice was not heeded because the CIA's less optimistic analysis swayed the administration.[152] Zhivkov's conduct on the international scene still suggested that he was heavily influenced by Soviet prompting.[153] In 1978, the poisoning in London, of the Bulgarian defector, writer, and broadcaster for the BBC World Service, RFE, and DW, Georgi Markov, gave new meaning to the words "Bulgarian umbrellas" and generated major disquiet in Washington.[154] The Carter administration dealt with the matter discretely through diplomatic channels,[155] but the affair revealed the complexity of Bulgaria's destabilizing role on the international scene.[156] Zhivkov's contrary behavior meant that many avenues for change could not be explored even when he improved cooperation by, for example, impeding narcotics trafficking and apprehending terrorists while Yugoslavia did not.[157]

Balkan cooperation presented problems to the United States. Brzezinski's tweaks of differentiation and emphasis on human rights prompted a steadily more confrontational U.S.S.R. to pay more attention to Balkan developments, limiting the United States' scope to deploy differentiation effectively. It also sought to make mischief in NATO's Achilles' heel, the Southern Flank, by exploiting the fact that Carter maintained the United States' chronic inability to mediate effectively between its two NATO allies because it needed to prioritize containment.[158] A Soviet "charm offensive" towards Greece and Turkey was pursued with vigor. Both reciprocated, but without compromising their Western

---

150 *FRUS* 1977–1980, XX, document 95.
151 Ibid, XX, document 90.
152 Ibid., document 90.
153 Ibid., document 88; Aurel Braun, *Small State Security in the Balkans* (London: Macmillan, 1983).
154 Richard H. Cummings, *Cold War Radio: The Dangerous History of American Broadcasting in Europe, 1950–1989* (Jefferson: McFarland and Company, 2009), 58–80; Rufus Crompton and David Gall, "Georgi Markov: Death in a Pellet," *Medico-Legal Journal* 48 (1980) 2: 51–62.
155 *FRUS* 1977–1980, XX, document 88.
156 Ibid., document 94.
157 Ibid., documents 94 and 95.
158 Athanasios Antonopoulos, *Redefining Greek–US relations, 1974–1980: National Security and Domestic Politics* (London: Palgrave Macmillan, 2020), 133–208; Aylin Güney, "The USA's Role in Mediating the Cyprus Conflict: A Story of Success or Failure?" *Security Dialogue* 35 (2004) 1: 27–42.

ties.¹⁵⁹ By the mid-1970s, Turkey had emerged as one of the top non-communist recipients of Soviet aid in the form of technical and economic assistance and from 1980 on Soviet energy too.¹⁶⁰ The fall of the Shah in Iran in January 1979 and the Soviet invasion of Afghanistan in December led to the Carter Doctrine in January 1980. Turkey, "the eternal barrier," was earmarked for additional aid in 1980. Greece was reintegrated into NATO in October 1980 before what the State Department called the "anti-NATO party of Andreas Papandreou" came to power.¹⁶¹ In a setting in which relations were already intricate, Carter's foreign policy, with its inflexible application of differentiation and its human rights message, left the communist Balkan states as well as Greece and Turkey nonplussed.

For a stratified differentiation policy to work, it needed support from and coordination with the United States' European allies. By this time, the Europeans sensed that détente was slipping away and were less than forthcoming. They worried that too much attention to human right abuses in the Soviet bloc would end up stoking Soviet tensions, undermine the pledges of Helsinki, and adversely affect the EEC's trading relations with Romania and Bulgaria.¹⁶² West German unhappiness with U.S. covert operations from Germany also made Chancellor Helmut Schmidt express his discomfort over the activities of the RFE/RL and the lack of German control over them.¹⁶³

President Reagan was to supercharge differentiation with bombastic rhetoric in which 'human rights' were employed as an overt "roll-back" weapon.¹⁶⁴ Such a policy in an area like the Balkans could have easily ossified the status quo. The region did not react well to the application of "maximum pressure." The rise of the Second Cold War in the 1980s, and Reagan's implementation of an accelerated differentiation led to intensified cooperation in the Balkans. Even Bulgaria shifted to multilateralism and would embark, with Greece and Romania, on initiatives to make the Balkans a 'nuclear free zone.'¹⁶⁵ In Greece, Papandreou, who knew how to win elections, also knew that NATO was the only guarantor of Greek security. Despite his being a thorn in the side of NATO with his "foot-

---

159 *FRUS 1977–1980*, XX, document 37.
160 International Institute for Strategic Studies, *Strategic Survey 1977* (London: IISS, 1978), 64–68.
161 *FRUS 1977–1980*, XXI, document 21.
162 Christian P. Peterson, "The Carter Administration and the Promotion of Human Rights in the Soviet Union, 1977–1981," *Diplomatic History* 38 (2014) 3: 628–56.
163 *FRUS 1977–1980*, XX, documents 52 and 54.
164 National Security Decision Directive (NSDD) 54, *United States Policy toward Eastern Europe*, 2 September 1982, Ronald Reagan Presidential Library <https://www.reaganlibrary.gov/public/archives/reference/scanned-nsdds/nsdd54.pdf> (1 September 2021).
165 Dragostinova, *The Cold War from the Margins*, 94.

notes,"¹⁶⁶ in the end, as Nils Ørvik observed, by 1984 Greece "belonged to the West much more than it had in 1974."¹⁶⁷ Papandreou made virtue of ambiguity by dressing it in fiery anti-NATO, anti-EEC, and nationalist rhetoric that allowed him to achieve a landslide electoral victory in 1981.¹⁶⁸ Romania continued to play the system at a time when its debt was spiraling, and would continue closer cooperation with Greece and Bulgaria, while Yugoslavia became increasingly introspective and less active in regional politics as it attempted to map out an uncertain future without Tito. Maneuvering continued until the end of the Cold War, and many of the Balkan countries would use their experiences of local détentes in the 1970s and the 1980s to assemble the framework for future post-Cold-War relations despite the instability caused by the Balkans Wars of the 1990s.

IX. Conclusion

For the Americans, the major interest in the Balkans was in its geostrategic location. The United States did not design the policy of differentiation exclusively with the communist Balkans states in mind, but it was where it was first tested and refined. Its legacy there was deeply contradictory. Although access to Western credit offered the prospect of attaining aspirations, in the long run this also opened the door to "walking into a debt trap."¹⁶⁹ Moreover, its effects could not be contained within its target countries but radiated out to influence U.S. allies too. The policy ran more smoothly during the High Cold War when it was conceived and designed. Its combination with détente proved to be trickier and even dangerous. The two policies were contradictory in nature and their effects incompatible. Their concurrent application proved to be unsettling for Balkan states across the Cold War divide. They acted as millstones, grinding down their national ambitions and priorities, provoking consecutive bouts of regional co-operation which went as far as they could in a region where suspicion and the Cold War acted as barriers. The constant balancing and unpredictable behavior of Balkan governments during this period revealed the internal contradictions of a policy that was supposed to promote change imperceptibly. The successes of

---

166 Pedaliu, "Footnotes", 237–58.
167 Nils Ørvik, *Semialignment and Western Security* (London: Groom Helm, 1986), 1–14.
168 Eirini Karamouzi, "'Out With the Bases of Death': Civil Society and Peace Mobilization in Greece During the 1980s," *Journal of Contemporary History* 56 (2021) 3: 617–38; Eirini Karamouzi and Dionysios Chourchoulis, "Troublemaker or Peacemaker? Andreas Papandreou, the Euromissile Crisis, and the Policy of Peace, 1981–86," *Cold War History* 19 (2019) 1: 39–61.
169 Berend, "What is Central and Eastern Europe?" 401–16.

differentiation are not easy to measure. Its aim was to keep nationalism alive behind the 'Iron Curtain'. In the Balkan region, where calculations were based more on realism, nationalism, and cynicism and less on ideology, this was not a difficult task. How far can one credit differentiation and nationalism for the end of the Cold War? It seems more plausible to maintain that the collapse of the U.S.S.R. was due to its failure to provide for the needs and hopes of its people, its reliance on fear to conceal its limitations, and its resorting to abusing the civil liberties and human rights of its own citizens. In this sense, credit needs to go to the policy of containment rather than one of its individual strategy strands.

Mišo Kapetanović

Yugoslav Labor Migrants Emerging as the Austrian Working Class (1960–1980)

I. Introduction

This article deals with class politics concerning Yugoslav labor migrants in Austria from the perspective of the Yugoslav state. Following Brigitte Le Normand's conceptualization of Yugoslav *gastarbajteri* as the transnational working class,[1] I investigate how the Yugoslav state dealt with issues associated with the class position of Yugoslav workers in Austria (employment, housing, access to services, and their resulting social mobility).[2] I explore these issues by examining documents related to bilateral meetings on the highest level as well as individual contacts between state officials. In doing so, I focus on the period from the signing of the agreement on equal employment rights for the workers and the convention regulating their social and health insurance up to the 1982, when labor migration politics changed course due to the influence of the campaign of the Organization for Security and Co-operation in Europe (OSCE) for organized return, and the Yugoslav state reduced economic privileges for the returning labor migrants.[3] I examine how the Yugoslav state understood the social position of its labor migrants and how advocacy of the migrants' interests was affected by cultural relations predating the bilateral relationship between the post-war states.

---

1 Brigitte Le Normand, "The Gastarbajteri as a Transnational Yugoslav Working Class," in *Social Inequalities and Discontent in Yugoslav Socialism*, edited by Rory Archer, Igor Duda, and Paul Stubbs (London: Routledge, 2016), 50–69.
2 I use the Serbo-Croat (*sh.*) version of the German-language term for labor migrants *Gastarbeiter* (guest worker). This version was abandoned in the German language due to implicit lack of integration of the "guests," but in Serbo-Croat, the term was adopted and is used to identify the demographics and culture behind it in the struggle for recognition within both the sending and the receiving communities.
3 Sara Bernard, *Deutsch Marks in the Head, Shovel in the Hands and Yugoslavia in the Heart: The Gastarbeiter Return to Yugoslavia (1965–1991)* (Wiesbaden: Harrassowitz Verlag, 2019); Sara Bernard, "Oil Shocks, Migration and European Integration: A (Trans)National Perspective on the Yugoslav Crises of the 1980s," *National Identities* 21 (2019) 5: 472.

Yugoslav society was organized following the idea of social justice and social mobility; interwoven with the ideology of brotherhood and unity, self-management, and non-alignment, it was proclaimed to be classless.[4] Recognizing class segregation or even distinction was ideologically problematic, yet class differences existed and were addressed.[5] The stratification of Yugoslav society was based on education, employment, and proximity to the party and the state, shifting class power from material means to an ability to instrumentalize the state. From the 1960s onwards, social differences became evident in housing and employment gaps.[6] These differences are connected to labor migration from Yugoslavia, even though migration cannot be reduced to employment, but is also motivated by better life opportunities, political affiliations, and ideas about society.[7] Yugoslav labor migrants were predominantly uneducated and from a rural background. They included a smaller proportion of skilled and highly skilled workers,[8] but the image of Yugoslav *gastarbajteri* is directly associated with their majority population.

In Austria, *gastarbajteri* occupied predominantly unqualified and manual labor positions. They took the modest housing spaces and a marginal position in the social life of the receiving society – in short, the lower ranks of the working classes. Austrian society was organized in a more traditional division between classes, in which social class was attributed to heritage and material means dating back to the imperial period. While some believe that post-war economic prosperity saw the classes became obsolete due to the evident growth of the middle-classes, they consolidated as interests around political parties.[9] This process is to be challenged, as migration will demonstrate how the decline of the Austrian

---

4 Dejan Jović, *Yugoslavia: A State That Withered Away* (West Lafayette: Purdue University Press, 2009).
5 Milovan Đilas, *The New Class: An Analysis of the Communist System* (London: Thames and Hudson, 1957); Đoko Stojičić,"Radnička klasa i kultura," *Kultura* 23 (1973): 214–20; Miroslav Živković, *Prilog jugoslovenskoj urbanoj sociologiji* (Beograd: Zavod za organizaciju poslovanja i obrazovanje kadrova, 1981).
6 Miroslav Živković, "Jedan Primer Segregacije u Razvoju Naših Gradova," *Sociologija* 10 (1968) 3: 37–58; Susan L. Woodward, *Socialist Unemployment: The Political Economy of Yugoslavia, 1945-1990* (Princeton: Princeton University Press, 1995); Brigitte Le Normand, "11. Yugoslavia," in *East Central European Migrations During the Cold War*, edited by Anna Mazurkiewicz (Berlin/ Boston: De Gruyter Oldenbourg, 2019), 368–95.
7 Ulf Brunnbauer, "Labor Emigration from the Yugoslav Region from the Late 19th Century until the End of Socialism: Continuities and Changes," in *Transnational Societies, Transterritorial Politics: Migrations in the (Post-) Yugoslav Region 19th–21th Century*, edited by Ulf Brunnbauer (München: Oldenbourg, 2009), 17–50.
8 Brigitte Le Normand, *Citizens without Borders: Yugoslavia and Its Migrant Workers in Western Europe* (Toronto Buffalo: University of Toronto Press, 2021), 31.
9 Anton Pelinka, *Out of the Shadow of the Past* (New York: Routledge, 1998), 97–128.

white working classes would be substituted with workers from the Balkans and outside of Europe, constructed as "other", or as less white whites.[10]

As class and its reproduction remained problematic categories in the language of the Yugoslav administration, even when discussed they were not admitted in the form of social policy. The article takes a closer look at how the question of class was approached from the perspective of the Yugoslav state by examining the documents produced by the Yugoslav side in negotiations with Austria. Seeking to identify the problem among the producers of these documents – the state officials (negotiators, top-ranking politicians, and diplomats) – I am interested in articulations about workers and the working class and transitions between workers and national minorities, as a translation from a social to a national issue. Observing the state of the art, I find that the cultural dimensions of these transfers are not explored. Often, the elephant in the room during negotiations was the question of the unspoken cultural hegemony of the former imperial center (Austria) and its former periphery (northern Yugoslavia). The hegemonic cultural relationship translated into questions of conduct, barbaric or civilized behavior, and the relevance of labor migrant problems where occasional incidents of workers' anti-social behavior predated questions of workers' rather material social needs (e.g. female workers' right to extend social insurance to their children).

The article is organized in five main sections. The following section provides a short overview of Yugoslav labor migration to Austria and its most important characteristics, followed by a survey of the important studies by Yugoslav and international scholars, and presentation of the sources. The third section provides a closer examination of the problem of class and how this question is articulated in the documents produced by Yugoslav actors. The fourth part deals with Yugoslav approaches and assumptions about the priorities of the Austrian side, demonstrating the presence of a cultural hegemonic relationship that outlived the redefinition of the modern state. The final section considers the labor migrants' responses to their situation, and the gradual but thorough shift from labor to ethnicity and national minority issues.

II. Détente and Labor Migration

The debates surrounding the Cold War détente of the 1960s and 1970s do not focus particularly on the questions of class, or even national minorities. If taken into consideration at all, labor migration is traditionally seen in the context of other large processes that unfolded in the period, such as the oil shocks and the

---

10 Maria N. Todorova, *Imagining the Balkans* (New York: Oxford University Press, 1997).

economic crisis of the 1970s, resulting in mass layoffs for the flexible labor force and a temporary return to Yugoslavia.[11] Yet the process of détente may be used to reveal how the social issue translated into a political one, in terms of labor migrants viewing specific states as potential allies – famously, Croatian nationals' expectations of the German state[12] – and how the individual states of Yugoslavia and Austria maneuvered these alliances in maintaining their priorities. More importantly, the macro-process of détente may help to reveal how the unarticulated question of class was substituted by the nation in the Yugoslav context and was largely ignored in the case of Austria.

Due to the bilateral nature of the relationship which defined post-war Austria and Yugoslavia as two independent nation states and equal partners, at least on the formal level, the current studies do not tackle the post-colonial dimension of this relationship. Although only Bosnia and Herzegovina (henceforth Bosnia) had been an Austro-Hungarian colony and only for only for a short time (1878–1918),[13] the northern half of Yugoslavia was an integral part of the empire. The imperial relationship between Austria and its former territories Slovenia, Croatia, Bosnia, and Vojvodina, involved an advanced form of multi-culturalism, but it was not free from cultural dominance from the imperial centers (Vienna, Budapest) and colonial relationships with regard to knowledge production, education, modernization, etc. The Austrian Empire was a first source of early modernization in the region, including those parts of later Yugoslavia that were never part of it (Montenegro, Kosovo, Macedonia). Ironically, after the formation of Yugoslavia, and particularly during the socialist period, the anti-colonial and anti-imperial sentiment in Yugoslavia took aim at the Ottoman Empire, and less at the Habsburgs.[14] The colonial relationship was not disintegrated by the so-

---

11 Sara Bernard, "Oil Shocks, Migration and European Integration," in Sara Bernard, "Developing the Yugoslav Gastarbeiter Reintegration Policy," in 5. Working Paper. Centre for Southeast European Studies, University Graz, 2012 <https://suedosteuropa.uni-graz.at/en/publications/working-papers/2012/developing-the-yugoslav-gastarbeiter-reintegration-policy> (30 July 2021).
12 Mate Nikola Tokić, "Landscapes of Conflict: Unity and Disunity in Post-Second World War Croatian Émigré Separatism," *European Review of History: Revue européenne d'histoire* 16 (2009) 5: 739–53; Petar Dragišić, "Hrvatska politička emigracija i Jugoslavija početkom osamdesetih godina. Pripreme za završni obračun," *Istorija 20. Veka* 38 (2020) 2: 203–18.
13 Clemens Ruthner (et al.) (eds.), *WechselWirkungen: Austria-Hungary, Bosnia-Herzegovina, and the Western Balkans, 1878–1918* (New York: Peter Lang Publishing Inc, 2015); Clemens Ruthner and Tamara Scheer (eds.), *Bosnien-Herzegowina und Österreich-Ungarn, 1878–1918. Annäherungen an eine Kolonie* (Tübingen: Narr Francke Attempto, 2018).
14 Initially the Austro-Hungarian period was qualified as 'dungeon of the people' (*sh.* – tamnica naroda) with pro-Serbian historians like Vladimir Ćorović vocally arguing against the Austrian regime (Vladimir Čorovic, *Bosna i Hercegovina* (Beograd:Graficki zavod" Makarije", 1925). The term lost its attachment over the years and today is equaly used for Yugoslavia (Ivo Goldstein, "Jugoslavija–idealan državni okvir, umjetna tvorevina ili tamnica naroda? (s posebnim obzirom na Hrvatsku i Bosnu i Hercegovinu)," *Forum Bosnae* 35 (2006): 90–104.

cialist revolution, and Vienna, Austrian society and Austrian culture play a dominant role in the post-imperial imaginary of culture and civilization.[15]

Michael Portmann states that the historical space of southeastern Europe was traditionally seen as a space of German (Austrian) domination.[16] Beyond the imperial tendencies, Austria was also an important center for the region in terms of the Enlightenment Movement, knowledge production, and export of cultural trends.[17] It is the dynamics of the relationship that remains underexplored even though primary sources as well as some works by other researchers report on host state actors' understandings of the culture, organization, and mentality of the migrants serving as a foundation for (discriminatory) policies. For example, Vladimir Ivanović cites a debate around the Croatian National Committee's attacks on the Yugoslav Ambassador Klarić in Bonn in 1966, where the German authorities were debating whether or not to provide further support to the CNC, and one of the arguments used to justify the attack was the hot-blooded, southern temper of the Croats.[18] The relationship between migrants and locals should therefore be seen and analyzed as a post-colonial relationship, analogous to the arrival of Caribbean workers in the United Kingdom and France[19] or workers from North Africa to post-war France.[20]

---

15 Frederick Cooper and Ann L. Stoler, *Tensions of Empire: Colonial Cultures in a Bourgeois World* (Berkeley: University of California Press, 1997); Harald Tiné and Michael Mann, *Colonialism as Civilizing Mission: Cultural Ideology in British India* (London: Anthem Press, 2004); Anne McClintock, *Imperial Leather: Race, Gender, and Sexuality in the Colonial Contest* (New York: Routledge, 1995); Hussein Alatas, *The Myth of the Lazy Native: A study of the image of the Malays, Filipinos and Javanese from the 16th to the 20th Century and its function in the ideology of Colonial Capitalism* (London New York: Routledge, 2010).
16 Michael Portmann, "Austria and Yugoslavia: Paths of a Difficult Neighborhood, 1955–1991," in *Peaceful Coexistence or Iron Curtain? Austria, Neutrality, and Eastern Europe in the Cold War and Détente, 1955–1989*, edited by Arnold Suppan and Wolfgang Mueller (Wien: Lit Verlag, 2009), 435–64.
17 On Austrian civilizing mission please see Werner Telesko, "Colonialism without Colonies: The Civilizing Missions in the Habsburg Empire," in *Cultural Heritage as Civilizing Mission: From Decay to Recorvery*, edited by Michael Falser (Switzerland: Springer International 2015), 35–48.
18 Vladimir Ivanović, *Geburtstag pišeš normalno. Jugoslavenski gastarbajteri u Austriji i SR Nemačkoj 1965–1973* (Beograd: Institut za savremenu istoriju, 2012), 180.
19 Margaret Byron and Stéphanie Condon, *Migration in Comparative Perspective: Caribbean Communities in Britain and France* (London: Routledge, 2008); Gary P. Freeman,, "Caribbean Migration to Britain and France: From Assimilation to Selection," in *The Caribbean Exodus*, edited by Barry B. Levine (New York: Praeger, 1987), 185–203.
20 Driss Maghraoui, "French Identity, Islam, and North Africans: Colonial Legacies. Postcolonial Realities," in *French Civilization and Its Discontents: Nationalism, Colonialism, Race* edited by Tyler Stovall and Georges Van den Abbeele (Lanham: Lexington Books, 2003), 213–235; Geoffroy de Laforcade, "Racialization and Resistance in France: Postcolonial Migrants, Besieged Cityscapes, and Emergent Solidarities," *WorkingUSA* 9 (2006) 4: 389–405.

The number of Yugoslav workers in Austria increased dramatically after 1965, when the two countries signed treaties regulating employment.[21] The treaties opened the Austrian labor market to Yugoslav workers, and the convention on social insurance made them equal to their Austrian counterparts with regard to employment and social security. The labor migration had already been flowing through informal channels from the early 1960s onwards and included an estimated 2,500, mostly male workers. The illegal migrants did not only come from border areas such as Slovenia and northern Croatia but also included workers from southern Croatia, Herzegovina, and northwestern Bosnia. The numbers increased intensively in the late 1960s. As early as 1967, there were up to 88,000 Yugoslav workers in Austria, and the numbers peaked in 1973 with as many as 150,000 workers. As the oil shocks reduced the demand for labor,[22] resulting in layoffs and the return of some workers, the numbers remained stable, with around 200,000 Yugoslavs living in Austria up to the beginning of the war in 1991.

Arriving groups of Yugoslavs met a diverse population in the receiving communities. Besides the majority, German-speaking Austrians, there were migrant workers from other countries, notably Turkey and Italy, and other Yugoslavs: political émigrés[23] who had found refuge in Austria, Yugoslav citizens of German descent who became Austrian citizens after their expulsion from socialist Yugoslavia, and Austrian national minorities with historical ties to individual Yugoslav republics. This last group included the Slovene national minority from Carinthia and to a lesser extent in Styria, and the Croat national minority in the Burgenland. However, the incoming labor migrants were the largest of the groups with ties to Yugoslavia, the most prominent and the least integrated into Austrian society, and not well connected to any of the above-mentioned groups.

The treaties intended for incoming labor to be regulated via the employment offices, but the majority of migrants (approximately two-thirds) came through informal channels, entering Austria on tourist visas and then looking for employment.[24] The result was chain migration and an uneven distribution of migrants throughout the country, with a concentration in the industrial urban

---

21 Agreement for the implementation of the Convention of 19 November 1965 between the Republic of Austria and the Socialist Federal Republic of Yugoslavia on social security, in *Bundesgesetzblatt*, 29 December 1966, text 290, no. 90; Convention (with final protocol) between the Republic of Austria and the Socialist Federal Republic of Yugoslavia on social security, in: *Bundesgesetzblatt*, 29 December 1966, text 289, no. 90.
22 Bernard, "Oil Shocks, Migration and European Integration".
23 In contrast to other emigration destinations such as Germany or France, Austria had a strong presence of Croat anti-Yugoslav émigrés, but there were not many Serb anti-Yugoslav elements. This could be explained by the proximity of Austria, and the pre-socialist ties of the Serb nationalists in France, the UK, and North America.
24 Ivanović, *Geburtstag pišeš normalno*.

centers and clusters of migrants from the same sending communities. The informal distribution somewhat responded to the informal needs of the economy and resulted in the clustering of large communities in the major centers (Vienna, Linz, Wels, Salzburg, Graz, Innsbruck). The chain migration also directed a gradual change of incoming migrants. Labor migrants from Slovenia and Croatia initially constituted the majority of the Yugoslav migrants. Through the late 1960s and the early 1970s they were outpaced by migrants from Bosnia and Serbia.[25] Yet this statistical trend should not be understood too literally. Through the interviews I learned that in Vienna there was a strong presence of Bosnian migrants even predating the Agreement and the Convention, and statistics show that majority of the Slovene migrants were more mobile, with higher return rates.

Arriving migrants were in a precarious position. As unqualified and manual laborers, they tended to end up in lower-paying jobs exposed to the informal economy and with little state protection. Outside of the employment and protection of the state treaties, they had to make their own way when looking for housing and organizing their social lives. Likewise, the migrants were not present in worker bodies or political representation.[26] As a matter of fact, the Yugoslav state discouraged the migrants from participating in the political life of the receiving communities, namely labor unions and political parties.[27] From the 1970s onwards, Yugoslavia became a crucial actor in supporting the organization of migrants in Yugoslav cultural and sport clubs. As Nikola Baković shows in the case of Germany – but it also applies to Austria – these clubs were essential in organizing labor migrants' social life, but were also an important tool for the Yugoslav state monitoring of citizens abroad.[28]

Ending up in lower paying jobs and not knowing the language made migrants' participation in society rather tough. As I argue in the third section of this article, the local resistance was not only a result of contemporary social dynamics between two demographics, but was also historically situated. The relationship

---

25 Le Normand, *Citizens without Borders*.
26 Ljubomir Bratić, "Soziopolitische Organisationen der MigrantInnen in Österreich," *Kurswechsel* 1 (2000): 6–20.
27 Ljubomir Bratić, "Soziopolitische Netzwerke der MigrantInnen aus der ehemaligen Sozialistischen Föderativen Republik Jugoslawien (SFRJ) in Österreich," in *Österreichischer Migrations- Und Integrationsbericht: Demographische Entwicklungen – Sozioökonomische Strukturen – Rechtliche Rahmenbedingungen*, edited by Heinz Fassmann and Irene Stacher (Klagenfurt: Drava Verlag, 2003), 395–409.
28 Nikola Baković, "Tending the 'Oasis of Socialism': Transnational Political Mobilization of Yugoslav Economic Emigrants in the FR Germany in the Late 1960s and 1970s," *Nationalities Papers* 42 (2014) 4: 674–90; Brigitte Le Normand, "Weaving a Web of Transnational Governance: Yugoslav Workers Associations," in *Citizens without Borders: Yugoslavia and Its Migrant Workers in Western Europe* (Toronto Buffalo: University of Toronto Press, 2021), 137–64.

between the local Austrians and the incoming Yugoslav workers was one of inherited hegemony between the former imperial metropolis and its provinces.

Rather, I argue that interactions between societies and individual groups affect their respective states and therefore bilateral relations. There is a need to examine how the historical position of the imperial metropolis and migrants arriving from the former provinces brought additional weight to the ways the migrants were perceived and treated. Vienna, as an imperial, and later national metropolis witnessed many migrant groups before and after Yugoslav labor migration, demonstrating different levels of acceptance, and hence the occasional hostility or racist treatment that Yugoslavs experienced was not unique. Yet the rapid racialization of *gastarbajteri* (both Yugoslav and Turkish) and social segregation indicates the possibility that this relationship resonated with the social dynamics of the incomers from the former imperial territories and locals who considered themselves more modern if not more civilized and culturally superior. These dynamics, largely unspoken and unarticulated, did exist and influenced the bilateral relationship.

I focus exclusively on the Yugoslav sources to learn how the Yugoslav state navigated the challenges of articulating and acting on the class position of its citizens abroad when it was not articulating it at home, and how this avoidance of class resulted in racialized thinking about the Yugoslavs themselves, or motivated individual groups to split from that collectivity. The article is based on research in the Fonds of the Archives of Yugoslavia in Belgrade, focusing on the fonds of the Yugoslav Communist Party, the Cabinet of the President of the Republic, the Federal Labor Council (1967–1971), the Federal Labor and Social Policy Secretariat (1971–1974), the Federal Labor and Employment Committee (1974–1978), and the Federal Committee for Labor, Health Care, and Social Protection (1974–1989). Documents from these fonds serve as the foundation for the analysis, which was additionally supported by interviews with members of the Knežević family conducted in June 2021, and two other families whose members migrated to Vienna from Bosnia in mid-1960s.

III. Class in the Migration Treaties

The analyzed documents from the above-mentioned fonds do not refer to class in the context of the bilateral agreements organizing labor migration. These documents discuss specific questions related to employment such as informal employment, or individual benefits. Class in political and social contexts is mentioned outside of bilateral agreements, such as in the documents providing political analysis of the individual political parties or political analysis in other countries used in exchange with Austrian Communist Party Officials. However, some of the fonds dealing with bilateral labor agreements also included rather specific individual documents pertaining to the social position of the Yugoslav workers, as was the case with a translation of an article containing detailed discussion of the realities faced by a Yugoslav family living in Vienna.

The questions that are related to class and that the Yugoslav side raised in the bilateral meetings are employment and labor-related social and health protection. These problems include informal employment (tourist visas), avoidance of Yugoslav employment offices, inadequate protection of informally employed workers, inadequate health and social support for injured workers, and child support for unmarried or divorced women. Some problems related to class but not directly connected to labor such as housing are not discussed in detail but left to the discretion of the Austrian housing system (a mixture of private, social, and state housing). But other indirectly related issues such as workers' free time and leisure were raised by both sides and discussed on more than one occasion.[29]

For the Yugoslav side, the most important problem concerning labor migration was the problem of informal employment. The informal employment predated the bilateral agreement, with previously mentioned estimates of around 2,500 individuals leaving Yugoslavia to Austria for employment in the early 1960s. With the Yugoslav state starting to issue passports to its citizens from 1960 onwards,[30] and Austria removing visas for Yugoslav passport holders the following year, the number of individuals leaving for Austria on a tourist visa to look for a job there directly rose steadily. The bilateral agreements were supposed to provide a legal framework and formalize secure migration, but the use of informal channels remained a continuous source of discontent on the Yugoslav side.

The question of "tourist" unemployment was raised most prominently during the meetings, particularly by the Joint Steering Committee for the Convention on Social Insurance. The Committee in question was founded as an extension of the employment agreement. The two sides represented on the Committee met once a year to discuss the implementation of the treaties. It was another channel for the Yugoslavs to voice their concerns, but it had limited success. In several instances

---

29 "Prevod članka" – translation of an untitled critical article from *Salzburger Nachrichten*, 27.08.1971, arguing about among other things the unorganized free time of the workers, 27 October 1971, Savezni sekretarijat za inostrane poslove, Beograd, 1971, 598-46-81, Arhiv Jugoslavije (AJ), Beograd; Izveštaj Jugoslovenske delegacije sa drugog sastanka Mešovite komisije predviđene sporazumom od 19. novembre 1965. godine između SFR Jugoslavije i Republike Austrije o regulisanju zapošljavanja jugoslovenskih radnika u Austriji koji je održan u Beogradu, od 7. do 11. maja 1973. godina, 25 May 1973, President of the Yugoslav delegation to the Steering Committee, Beograd, 1973, 2–3, 598–46–81, AJ, Beograd; Izveštaj o poseti savezno-g sekretara za rad i socijalnu politiku republici Austriji, 1 June 1973, Federal Secretary for Labor and Social Affairs, Beograd, 1973, 7, 598–46–81, AJ, Beograd.

30 Ivanović, *Geburtstag pišeš normalno*, 51.

throughout the period, the Yugoslav representatives concluded that the Austrian state was not doing enough to prevent informal employment of Yugoslav workers, concluding that the weak implementation of the agreement's rules was to protect Austrian employers.[31] A report from one of these meetings also concludes that this approach entailed social and economic risks for Yugoslav workers and directly accuses Austrian government of inaction.[32] The experiences of both official meetings and the Steering Committee demonstrate a difference in interpretation of the treaties, and an Austrian practical approach to acquiring labor which left Yugoslav workers exposed to social risks.

The question of informal employment is followed by a plethora of smaller questions regarding social protection of the workers. The Yugoslav side records an alarming number of cases in which workers were not protected by the agreement. These include lower salaries than the Austrian employees received for the same roles (especially in rare cases of qualified employment), inadequate accommodation, invalid taxation, and the inability to use social insurance or child support, or to extend medical insurance to family members in the case of female workers.[33] The immediate solution to these problems was the establishment of labor attachés by the Yugoslav diplomatic missions.

Outside of the fonds analyzed and researched in this project, class is referred to in the analyses of international politics, and in communication with the Communist Party of Austria (KPÖ).[34] Even there, class is referred to in general remarks about Austrian society, with respect to the conditions working class individuals were facing. In the context of the Yugoslav workers, the KPÖ complained about workers' political alliances; workers preferred the Social Democrats (SPÖ) to the Communists in the workers' councils.

Understanding of class and the social position of the workers exists even though it is not directly articulated. For example, in documents pertaining to the

---

31 Informacija o nekim pitanjima zapošljavanja jugoslovenskih građana u Austriji koja će biti predmet razgovora saveznog sekretara za rad i socijalnu politiku i ministra za socijalnu upravu Austrije, February 1973, Confidential, Beograd, 1973, 598–46–81, AJ, Beograd.
32 Izveštaj Jugoalovonako delegacije sa drugog sastanka Mešovite komisije predviđene sporazumom od 19. novembre 1965. godine između SFR Jugoslavije i Republike Austrije o regulisanju zapošljavanja Jugoslovenskih radnika u Austriji koji je održan u Beogradu, od 7. do 11. maja 1973. godina, 25.05.1973, President of the Yugoslav delegation to the Steering Committee, Beograd, 1973, 598–46–81, AJ, Beograd.
33 Informacija o osnovnim podacima i problemima zapošljavanja jugoslovenskih građana u Austriji, December 1974, Sektor za zaposlenost i zapošljavanje, Beograd, 1974, 577–24–31, AJ, Beograd.
34 Izveštaj o radu XX Kongresa Komunističke partije Austrije, u Beču od 3–6 januara 1969. Godine, 20 January 1969, Beograd, Danilo Kekić and Dževad Mujezinović, 507 IX, 6/I-264, AJ, Beograd.

Agreements,[35] I found a translation of an article about a Yugoslav family living in Vienna. The document's inclusion in the materials itself indicates that there was some awareness on the part of the Federal Executive Council that involved registering the article, translating it and distributing it among committees.

The article itself was written by the Viennese journalist Otto Fisher in 1971 and published in the left-leaning journal *Arbeiter Zeitung* on the occasion of Mother's Day, and was discernably titled "Ah, so Yugoslavs…" The protagonists of the story, the Knežević family, came to Vienna from rural Bosnia. Srećko, the father, came in the early 1960s, followed by Milojka (Mila), the mother, in 1966.[36] They met at work and married soon after. The road to the place they resided at the time the article was written was a tough one. Mila was expecting a second child while working as a kitchen assistant in a hospital. When her former employer found out she was pregnant with their first child, Robert, she was fired. The family had also lost modest accommodation after the landlord found out that the family would be expanding. The boy, Robert, then three-and-a-half, was sick and in a hospital due to chronic bronchitis, which the family attributed to the moldy, cold apartments they had previously been forced to live in.[37]

Focusing on the life circumstances of one family, Fischer tackles Vienna's unspoken antagonism towards the Yugoslavs. He ascribes it to the infamous Viennese snobbery and resentment. Fischer sees this resistance in the way the locals pronounce words such as Yugoslavs, Turks, or *Gastarbeiter* full of reservation when he is looking for the family's apartment. Fischer additionally illustrates the resistance by pointing out the lack of the family's name on the apartment door, in contrast to those of the neighbors. When he inquires about the family, the young neighbor does not know them, even though Milojka and Srećko were the buildings' maintenance personnel, but he knows that there are some Yugoslavs living in an apartment on the ground floor.[38] Fischer's article strongly suggests that Yugoslav labor migrants occupied the lower strata of the Austrian working class and are excluded from the state protection and social system via numerous examples of Milojka's and Srećko's struggle in the city.

Yet Fischer presents the family's story as both a struggle and a success. He describes the mother's good German with only a trace of a Serbian accent, and the

---

35 Bilaterlani sporazumi o zaštiti interesa jugoslovenskih radnika u Austriji: "Prevod članka Otto Fishera 'Ah, tako Jugosloveni…'", Beograd, 1971, 586–41–60, AJ, Beograd.
36 As exemplified by Srećko Knežević and two other families I had the opportunity to meet in June 2021, the fathers arrived in Austria via informal channels before the treaties were signed, to be followed by the mother, who joined them in the late 1960s. All three couples met in Vienna and emanated from northwestern Bosnia (Prnjavor in the case of the Kneževićs and Sanski Most and Glamoč in the other two).
37 "Prevod članka Otto Fishera 'Ah, tako Jugosloveni…'," 4586–41–60, AJ, Beograd.
38 Ibid., 2.

father's efforts to describe their situation despite his limited knowledge of the language.[39] This is contrasted with a story of the boy growing up in German surroundings, his parents speaking only German with him, and weak connections to the sending state, Yugoslavia.[40] Fischer assumes they have weak ties with Yugoslavia and the Yugoslav community in the city, and presents the Knežević family as having adapted quickly. According to Fischer, the reason for this rapid integration lies in family life, and the mother's efforts. But in a short reflection on the father's life before the marriage, Fischer qualifies Srećkos premarital existence through a "ghetto" of miserable workers' apartments, pitiful gatherings squatting[41] at the Südbahnhof, and "one-hour" love encounters in the Prater's red-light establishments.[42] Fischer thus paints a picture of the prevalent reality for many more "maladapted" workers existing on the margins of society.

Fischer's article is an important insight into the private and public spaces labor migrants occupy in Vienna in the early 1970s and their perception by the receiving society.[43] Five years after the signing of the agreement and the convention, Yugoslav labor migrants arrived in vast numbers and easily occupied spaces designated for them – the low prestige positions in unqualified and manual labor. The international documents did not define other aspects of social life important for class positions, for which housing and social spaces are important. The story of Mila illustrates labor migrants' inability to access adequate housing and their precarious position at work. But the short details from Srećko's pre-marital life illustrate the social standing of the incoming migrants in the public sphere. For male labor migrants from Yugoslavia, Vienna was restricted to work, communal workers' housing, and Sundays at the Südbahnhof. However, it is the resistance of the receiving community that Fischer reports on and his efforts to portray the Kneževićs as adapted that speak about the underlying hierarchy between the Viennese and the labor migrants that extends to the Austrians and the Yugoslavs.

What are the class-related logics at play here? The rapid arrival of the Yugoslav migrants in Austria was smaller in volume compared to Germany, but much

---

39 Ibid.
40 Ibid., 3.
41 These gatherings were grounds for reinvigorating the racialized slur "Tschusch" and associated with the practice of squatting common for both Slavic and southern European informal gatherings.
42 "Prevod članka Otto Fishera 'Ah, tako Jugosloveni…'," 6, 586–41–60, AJ, Beograd.
43 Vladimir Ivanović provides an overview of a perception of *gastarbajteri* in Vienna in 1971, based on a study *Gastarbeiter, Wirtschaftliche und soziale Herausforderungen* (Arbeitskreis für ökonomische und soziologische Studien, *Gastarbeiter, Wirtschaftliche und soziale Herausforderungen* (Wien: Europaverlag (et.al.), 1973)). In the study the Viennese see *gastarbajteri* as necessary evil, barbaric, destructive presence that is there to do the work but should not be mixed with the general population, *Geburtstag pišeš normalno*, 298.

more conspicuous. The newcomers created pressure on the city's infrastructure, which did not necessarily grow in step with labor demands. One should accept with reservation the explanation that the poor housing was due to greater demand. Considering that in the 1960s and the 1970s Vienna's population was in decline,[44] the explanation for the housing problems faced by the labor migrants should also be looked for elsewhere. In public, migrants occupied those spaces to which they had access – transitory public spaces such as the train station, the Prater, or other parks. They were noticeable only as a disorderly and noisy bunch.[45]

The arriving migrants were not only from a Yugoslav, but also from a rural background. Similar demographics were also reluctantly received in Yugoslav urban areas, or indeed any larger cities of the mid-twentieth century. In mid-century Austria, the word Yugoslav had a plurality of meanings, but most of them fell under the losing end of the East–West, rural–urban, barbaric–civilized, traditional–modern dichotomies. The result was middle-class resistance towards the newcomers occupying the margins of the society as working classes. In the following, I examine how the Yugoslav authorities dealt with the problems surrounding the labor migrants' arrival and positioning in Austrian society. The presence of this translation demonstrates that Yugoslav authorities were engaged in the question of social position even if they avoided calling it class.

IV. Preparing to meet the Austrians

As mentioned in the previous section, the members of the Yugoslav delegations were particularly wary that the Austrian side might bring up anti-social behavior allegedly committed by Yugoslav labor migrants in the cities. The Austrian side did not officially raise such issues, at least not on the highest level. In conversations about labor migration, the Austrian representatives focused on responding to the Yugoslav concerns rather than raising their own, even though the Yugoslav side was not always satisfied with the answers. But for the matters they did raise, there were obvious priorities and a focus on the needs of the demographics the two states advocated.

Rather interesting problems in the bilateral conversations were related to the culture and social acceptance of the workers in Austria, many of which remained undebated. The Yugoslav reports continuously informed their negotiators about a backlash within Austrian society towards Yugoslav labor migrants, cases of

---

44 *Statistische Jahrbücher der Stadt Wien* (Statistical Yearbooks of the City of Vienna) 1961 to 1980.
45 Ivanović, *Geburtstag pišeš normalno*, 299.

discrimination, and racial abuse. They occasionally also included the sensitive topic of migrants' anti-social behavior in public places (Serbo-Croat: *ispadi*). Anti-social behavior on the part of idle Yugoslav workers loomed over Yugoslav diplomats in late 1960s, and they were preparing for the Austrian side raising this question. The term *ispad*, literally meaning an outburst in Serbo-Croat, was used in several other contexts, most poignantly during the nationalist backlash against the Slovene-speaking minority in Carinthia. In state documents, the term was used to describe embarrassing as well as unacceptable behavior. But in the case of the labor migrants' rowdiness, the topic never arose in bilateral meetings despite constant Yugoslav fears and anticipation.

The Yugoslav diplomats' fear of talk about anti-social behavior on the part of labor migrants speaks of a deeper cultural relationship that involves shared knowledge beyond a mere labor transaction. It involved a shared understanding of civil behavior and decency, and with it images of cultural hierarchies that were relevant for an understanding of this fear. Anti-social behavior on the part of Yugoslav workers seems to be too embarrassing for both the Austrian and the Yugoslav side to talk about in the high-level meetings. Yet the reports narrow it down to unauthorized mass gatherings of workers in public spaces. One of these major incidents was a "Balkan Woodstock", described by Vladimir Ivanović, during which 3,500 Yugoslav workers met for picnics including a spit roast on the weekends in Vienna's Augarten.[46] The gatherings forced the city government to organize police raids to control unregistered events, but also to designate a space on the Danube Island where *Gastarbeiter* could meet and spend time.[47]

The intercultural setting of labor migrants' public misbehavior hides the fact that this type of conduct was also looked down upon in Yugoslavia, as it was in Austria when the country's rural population moved to the cities. *Ispadi* are an important symptom of how Yugoslav state officials perceived labor migrants and Yugoslavs in Austria. The migrants' conduct may have been reprehensible, but the narratives in the state documents speak about a culturized understanding of class related to the working men's and women's habitus.

The Yugoslav officials fear of the Austrian officials bringing up accusations of anti-social behavior was not unfounded. The tensions concerning the conduct of the Yugoslav migrants in public was a minor complaint addressed to the Yugoslav diplomatic staff at the Vienna embassy. The Austrian state dealt with the problem on its own terms, recognizing that it was not the Yugoslav government's responsibility to persuade their citizens to act acceptably. The alleged misbehavior was a consequence of the enforced idleness of the workers and the inability to create their social spaces or enter accessible leisure. The issue was

---

46 Ivanović, *Geburtstag pišeš normalno*, 240.
47 Ibid., 241.

further complicated by a lack of an integration policy until the 1980s but remained a feature of supporting documents in preparation for state visits.

The solution to anti-social behavior came in the form of the social clubs advocated by both sides. To solve the problems of the workers' free time and leisure, the Austrian officials suggested opening a small library or cultural center. The interesting insistence on libraries reveals a lack of insight into the needs and culture of the workers. Not even Yugoslav white-collar civil servants were particularly well-informed about the needs of the blue-collar workers. As later experience will show, the most successful arrangements related to entertainment, sports, and humanitarian organizations.

When raising problems of their own, the Austrian officials only mentioned the labor migrants when addressing the issues in the systems that involved them. For example, the Austrians complained about the overcrowded trains carrying numerous Yugoslav workers towards Austria, Germany, and Switzerland. The number of people on the trains is occasionally described as so excessive that it becomes impossible for the state border officials to enter and check the passengers. This issue is raised through the diplomatic channel in Belgrade, embassy official Erwin Matsch paying a visit to Jovan Polkić at the State Secretariat for Foreign Affairs and expressing their concern.[48]

The above-mentioned problems only marginally concern labor migrants. The problems related to the delayed trains; evidently, long waiting hours at border crossings are more a matter of leisure and the convenience of the border officials and tourists than a labor relations issue. Here the Austrian side is pursuing potential complaints by its citizens, and not any citizens, but those going on holiday to Croatia, a broad spectrum of Austrian society with a substantial chunk belonging to the middle classes who had access to leisure in Austria and in Yugoslavia.

With the growing prosperity of post-war social democracy in Austria, social class became a more hidden and unarticulated question. In contrast to the well-defined and -positioned social classes of the imperial times and interwar Austria, the so-called *Lager* system, the post-war economic growth brought prosperity with widely available consumer goods and an increase in the middle-classes.[49] Out of the political parties that actively visited Yugoslavia or invited Yugoslav representatives, only the representatives the Communist Party of Austria (KPÖ) spoke about divisions among classes, the class position of the workers, and an ongoing struggle, as various documents in the fonds show. As the Yugoslavs were

---

[48] Zabeleška o razgovoru, Beograd, 18 February 1970; official note of the Austrian Embassy in Belgrade, Belgrade, 16 February 1970 (Serbo-Croat translation), Belgrade, 1970, 586–41–60, AJ, Beograd.
[49] Pelinka, *Out of the Shadow of the Past*.

much more receptive towards KPÖ ideas about international politics, the Austrian Communists also complained about the lack of support from the Yugoslav workers, and an occasional lack of support on the part of the Yugoslav state. The marginalization of questions relating to the labor migrants in the bilateral agreements coincides with a decrease in the presence of the Austrian Communist Party in factories and other forms of public life.

The major parties (the Social Democrats (SPÖ), and the conservative Austrian People's Party (ÖVP)) did not raise the class question at all. They treated it as irrelevant, claiming that there were no classes in Austrian society. The Yugoslavs workers mainly supported the SPÖ and through this support accepted the party's narrative of equal opportunities. This period in Austrian history was also a period of social divisions between the Conservatives and the Social Democrats which produced dual systems (so-called *Proporz*) catering for the supporters of each party and fractured important political issues through the relevant debates between the two sides' articulations.[50]

The Yugoslav labor migrants struggled to be anything more than cheap labor and the Austrian state dealt with them as such. But in the sea of issues between the ÖVP and the SPÖ, the social position and mobility of the Yugoslav migrants were not relevant. The internal Yugoslav issues were the questions of the national minorities in Carinthia and the Burgenland, and in the mid-1970s Yugoslav accusations about Austria's alleged sheltering of anti-Yugoslav terrorists. The SPÖ took a more pro-Yugoslav stance in these debates (supporting Slovene minority rights and the Yugoslav state against the terrorists) and in exchange gained the support of the Yugoslav workers. The fact that this support weakened potential debates about class was simply irrelevant.

Like Turkish and other Southern European as well as non-European migrants, the Yugoslav migrants were an underclass that was ethnicized and racialized. As the upper classes (the former Habsburg nobility) disappeared from public life, the social divisions of interwar and post-war Austria were dominated by class-based political camps (*Lager*), defining the urban working classes as supporters of the Social-Democratic Party, and the middle classes and peasantry as supporters of the conservative Catholic conservative politics, carried by the Austrian People's Party. Growing middle-classes and turn towards service economy gave an impression of diminishing social classes, yet the "*Lager* mentality" began to decline towards the 1980s.[51] The focus on the political affiliation of the social class also overlooks how the lower strata of the working classes were increasingly confronted with incoming migration. The migrants might not have been citizens,

---

50 Ibid.
51 Fritz Plasser, Peter A. Ulram and Alfred Grausgruber, "The decline of 'Lager mentality' and the new model of electoral competition in Austria," *West European Politics* 15 (1992) 1: 16–44.

but they were a part of the local communities and society. The fact that their residence was considered temporary did not reduce their participation in the economy and local life. Treating the question of the classes as an internal Austrian question further marginalized labor migrants and moved the question beyond the political realm.

The Yugoslav state was aware of the problems related to the positions of the workers but also seemed to accept the political discourse set between the two main Austrian political parties. The reasons for this lay in pressure from other questions both external in negotiations with Austria and internal from the individual republics as well as in the understanding of cultural hierarchies that remained unarticulated in the documents. Between Yugoslavia and Austria, there were, and are, cultural hegemonies that were, and indeed still remain, unaddressed but which stem from the previous colonial relationships.

In the context of the labor migration, the existing cultural hegemony was further compounded by a rural–urban dimension – that is, Yugoslav workers coming from rural areas to the Austrian urban centers. Equally a legacy of the past, the post-colonial hegemonies structured cultural dynamics between the Austrian and the Yugoslav sides, as evident in the latter's fear of accusations of anti-social behavior as a relevant issue in bilateral exchanges. As the next section will show, cultural hegemonies were also manifested in the lack of understanding of the cultural needs of migrants on both sides, diplomats failing to acknowledge the cultural needs of the workers.

The Austrian representatives approached the problems the Yugoslavs raised with polite reservation and avoidance. They actively addressed problems that were relevant for their citizens and therefore might appear marginal from the perspective of labor migrants. The Austrian officials seem almost unaware of the labor migrants' difficulties, but the level of priority is the key factor when it comes to the refusal to recognize the existence of class. Examining the typology of these complaints, I argue that there was a difference in levels of priority given to the questions related to class.

V. Replacing class with nationality

The measures created by the agreements and negotiated by the states did not always work, and labor migrants were vocal about their positions. This section explores the role of the labor migrants in the process and how they engaged with the Yugoslav state. As both Austria and Yugoslavia increasingly saw labor migrants in terms of their nationality and therefore ethnicity rather than their social standing, this section shows how class-related issues gradually lost relevance and

Figure 1: "My name is Kolaric. Your name is Kolaric. Why are you called Tschusch?" This contemporary campaign condemned xenophobia referring to the fact that a lot of Austrians are descendants of immigrants (Source: Votava / Imagno / picturedesk.com)

labor migrants attempted to draw attention to their own issues, exemplified in a parodical case of a strike at the ESPA factory in Wilhelmsburg in 1978.

On 24 February 1978, twenty-seven Yugoslav workers employed in three shifts in the ESPA ceramic factory in Wilhelmsburg (Lower Austria) launched a general strike to show support for an Austrian foreman fired the previous day for intoxication and sleeping on the job.[52] The Yugoslav workers saw the foreman as an ally and acted immediately, even though he advised them not to. The workers had gone on strike once before, in 1977, when the company raised salaries for other workers but not the Yugoslavs, and had been successful in fighting for their interests. The company immediately fired them all, effectively ending the strike. After reporting substantial losses, the company later returned ten workers to work, to continue production in the third shift. The rest ended up unemployed and were banned from working in the municipality.[53]

---

52 Predmet: Štrajk naših radnika, 10 May 1978, Izveštaj, D. Lukić, Beč, 1971, 578–41–50, AJ, Beograd.
53 The workers reported to the Yugoslav diplomatic staff that the employment ban extended to Lower Austria, which was later established to be not true.

The Yugoslav officials treated the situation as a labor rights issue, but also as a semi-embarrassing matter that required damage control. The initial report vividly describes the Austrian foreman's intoxication.[54] The workers' methods are also presented in a negative light, for example in the sentence: "In order to 'stand together' in solidarity, there were even threats among our workers that whoever returned to work would be stabbed [...]."[55] The report also describes in some detail the moral fragility of the workers that came after the lay-offs, stating that those who had lost their jobs tried different methods to return to work such as "mutual accusations, bribing and paying the Austrians, moving things in a truck for another foreman and factory management."[56] The reservation and occasional cynicism of the diplomat in the reports is supported by didactic interventions. He claimed to have explained to the workers why the strike was not legitimate, emphasizing the cynical aspects of the workers' actions and their inability to understand and act in the situation.

Practical intervention on the part of the diplomatic officials came in response to the alleged loss of work permits for Lower Austria. Immediately after the lay-off, the workers found employment at a local ironworks and on the railway, though they could not obtain work permits due to the local employment ban. Upon being contacted, the embassy officials discovered that the prohibition in question referred to Wilhelmsburg only and was due to the strike's non-compliance with the Austrian Labor Union or Labor Chamber, and conducted meetings with the representatives from the regional branch of these organizations to remove the ban.[57]

The intervention was a success, leaving several clues as to the laborers' agency in the process. While occasionally humorous and limited in its impact, the Wilhelmsburg strike demonstrates how workers used the tools at their disposal to improve their position. This example also shows the exclusion of the workers from the local labor institutions (trade unions, the Labor Chamber, formal strikes) and their overreliance on the Yugoslav state representatives. The role of the Yugoslav representatives was not unilateral and remains debatable with respect to its patronizing relationship with and reservation towards the workers. But the case demonstrates how the categories of class and ethnicity figured in the negotiations.

In contrast to class, problems around ethnicity when it related to the workers are more easily identifiable in documents concerning the bilateral agreements

---

54 Ibid., 1.
55 Ibid.; Da bi se 'solidarno' držali zajedno, bilo čak pretnji među našim radnicima da onaj koji se bude vratio na posao biće izboden nožem…, 2, 578–41–50, AJ, Beograd.
56 Ibid., 2.
57 Predmet: Štrajk naših radnika, 8 June 1978, Izveštaj, D. Lukić, Beč, 1971, 578–41–50, AJ, Beograd.

and their negotiation. Ethnicity gained relevance with respect to two issues: the terrorist activities of émigrés escalating in 1972 and the issues related to the Yugoslav national minorities in Austria. I argue that these issues were a powerful distraction from the fact that neither the Austrian nor the Yugoslav representatives knew how to conceptualize and speak about the ongoing process of the labor migrants' social positioning. Due to the urgency of events related to the two issues, the question of migrants was put on the back burner and, in the longer historical process of bilateral negotiations, lost importance to them.

During the summer of 1972, the terrorist group Croatian Revolutionary Brotherhood (CRB) launched several attacks in Yugoslavia.[58] The organization was founded in Australia and organized in Western Europe, but their members entered Yugoslavia from Austria. After dealing with the attack in the August of 1972, Yugoslavia engaged in a campaign against the countries it perceived responsible for hosting the organization and its foundation. As Petar Dragišić notes, this campaign consisted of protest notes and harsh *aide memoires* addressed through diplomatic cables that put a heavy strain on bilateral relations.[59]

The incident reinforced suspicions about anti-Yugoslav émigrés in Austria that had existed since the end of the war and had a corresponding effect on relations between the two countries. Austria rejected the accusations and responded with criticism. The government denied any knowledge of such an operation, its main argument being the scale of Yugoslav migration to Austria; claiming it was impossible to monitor 150,000 individuals and thus using *gastarbajteri* as an excuse.[60]

The incident soured bilateral relations but resulted in more support for labor migrants. Of the policies that followed the incident, the most important was more support for the organization and foundation of Yugoslav clubs in Austria, this time without focusing on cultural activities and with larger oversight by the Yugoslav state. The measures involved neither the churches nor the national minorities in Carinthia and in the Burgenland. When the clubs later received criticism for serving as an instrument of the Yugoslav state in Germany,[61] the Austrian public and the state remained silent. The labor migrants condemning the terrorist attacks were not given much of a platform in the decision-making. The result was a larger push for Yugoslav clubs and more opportunity for Yugoslavia to interfere in this sphere, but it also meant Austria could outsource this problem.

---

58 Petar Dragišić, "Operation Phoenix in Yugoslavia in the Summer of 1972 and Yugoslav-Austrian Relations," *Tokovi Istorije* 26 (2018) 3: 87–106.
59 Ibid.
60 Ibid., 98.
61 Baković, "Tending the 'Oasis of Socialism'".

In the autumn of same year, nationalistic German-speaking groups in Carinthia engaged in the destruction of bilingual topographical signs (the so-called *Ortstafelsturm*). The action was seen as a threat in Yugoslavia and provoked another spate of protest notes, further destabilizing relations until 1974. Like other Yugoslavs, the labor migrants initially engaged with the story and were sympathetic to the cause of the Slovene minority in Carinthia. Yet this support shifted rather soon. A letter by ten representatives of Yugoslav clubs in Austria (and Germany) addressed to Yugoslav President Tito illustrates labor migrants' initial support and quick disillusionment.[62] The authors informed the state of their action to go to Carinthia to see the situation for themselves and show support for the Slovene minority, whom they perceived as Yugoslav. The visit did not prove to be a success. In the letter, the labor migrants vividly complain about the hostile and almost racist reception they received from the Slovene-speaking minority communities. The authors complain how instead of giving them a 'brotherly' reception, the villagers had turned their heads away from the Yugoslav group, while the children threw stones at them.[63] The correspondents then argue that their own status is precarious and complain that the Yugoslav state's support for the "hostile" minority is misguided.[64]

What the incident shows is that *gastarbajteri* saw and articulated unequal treatment by the state. Towards the 1970s, the labor migrants' background began to change from Slovenia and Croatia to Serbia, Bosnia, and other Yugoslav republics, including parts of Yugoslavia which had not been part of the Habsburg Empire. The expansion was reflected in the internal politics of Yugoslavia and power-sharing between its republics. The above-mentioned issues of terrorism and minorities were subjects of lobbying and sponsorship by the respective republics, Croatia in the first case, and Slovenia and Croatia in the second. The problems faced by labor migrants, on the other hand, appeared to be all-Yugoslav problems, but ultimately lacked a republic which would argue for their interests. A report for President Tito clearly indicates that the Republics of Slovenia and Croatia lobbied for greater importance to be attached to the causes they supported, raising the importance of these issues in bilateral meetings.[65]

Those migrants that came from former imperial territories such as Slovenia, Croatia, or Vojvodina in Serbia also sold themselves as culturally superior and more adapted to Austrian culture. Those that did not come from former imperial

---

62 Otvoreno pismo Gastarbajtera iz Austrije i Njemačke, 30 August 1970, Beograd, 1970, 837-I-5-b/4.5.6., AJ, Beograd.
63 Ibid.
64 Ibid.
65 Pregled važnijih pitanja u vezi sa razgovorima Pretsednika Republike druga Tita za vreme posete Austriji, 7 February 1967, State Secretariat for International Affairs, Belgrade, 1967, 6, 837 I-2/32, AJ, Beograd.

territories were subordinate in the hierarchy as less developed, less civilized, less organized, and less cultured. As the population of the labor migrants (*gastarbajteri*) shifted towards more southern parts of the Yugoslav state, so the term became increasingly associated with even less prestige, southern labor migrants being the lowest in the cultural hierarchy that also included émigrés and national minorities. The changes from the early 1970s onwards make the term *gastarbajteri* less relevant, but its new content implies that it should not be seen outside of the ethno-class dynamics, but with emphasis on class traits.

The question of cultural hegemony reflected the singular nationalistic grievances with the Yugoslav state and the personnel tasked with looking after labor migrants' interests. An interesting indicator for this situation was an off-the-cuff remark by Croatian revolutionaries in 1967 in a letter addressed to President Tito after his visit to Austrian president Franz Jonas.[66] Signing as "Croatian academics", a group of Croatian political émigrés complained about the rule of the Yugoslav state and the problem of Serb bureaucrats in embassies mistreating Croatian workers. To illustrate the point, they refer to the Serb bureaucrats using the slur "shepherds" (Serbo-Croat: *čobani*) to imply that they lack civility while Croats naturally belong to the Empire.[67] However, the term also reflects the Yugoslav urban mythology of the socialist period articulated against working classes coming from the rural areas.[68]

The issue of class was never far away from that of ethnicity and was connected to the physical distance from the former imperial metropolis. The lack of class, or the lack of symbolic capital implied by the "Croatian academics" demonstrates how ethnicization was used to challenge the Yugoslav project, in reaffirmation of the ethnic identity in the diaspora. By using the slur *čobani*, the authors of the letter imply that there is an understandable system of collectivities in which some Yugoslav labor migrants are worthy of Austrian respect due to their civility and cultivation. It also reaffirms the question as to how class was ethicized.

The terrorist attack of 1972 moved the attention of both states away from workers to the role of Yugoslav émigrés and treated labor migrants only as potential recruitment material for possible threats. The actions of the workers, even when they failed, as in the case of the visit to Carinthia's Slovene-speaking villages or the workers' strike in Wilhelmsburg in 1978 show that workers understood and acted in these processes but were left on the sidelines. When they demonstrated agency as workers (class) and not as citizens/nationals (Croats or Serbs), the state officials attached significantly less importance to workers. The

---

66 Otvoreno pismo pretsjedniku SFRJ Josipu Broz Tito, Dr. Vladimiru Bakarič, gosp. Janku Smole, 15 February 1967, Beč, 1967, 837 I-2/32, AJ, Beograd.
67 Ibid., 2.
68 Andrei Simić, *The peasant urbanites: A Study of Rural-Urban Mobility in Serbia* (New York and London: Seminar Press, 1973).

growing relevance of the national questions, including in bilateral relations, also reframed workers through their respective nationalities.

VI. Conclusion

The case of Yugoslav labor migrants is poignant, since it involves conspicuous demographics (up to 150,000 within a ten-year period) of overwhelmingly underqualified workers (85 % unqualified and some skilled manual laborers). Moving to the Austrian industrial centers, the Yugoslav rural demographics occupied positions of the lower working classes in Austria corresponding to those positions they would occupy in the social strata of Yugoslavia (rural-to-urban blue-collar worker-peasants). Class is not something that can be regulated via bilateral agreement, nor are changing class dynamics unique to the experience of Yugoslav labor migrants in Austria from 1960 to 1970, yet the early experience of the Yugoslav labor migrants had paved the way for future waves of migration and positioned the former Yugoslav labor migrants on the margins of Austrian society.

The problem with class lay in the Austrian government's reluctance to ensure the migrants had guaranteed access to full workers' rights and resistance on the part of the receiving society. This situation was a result of the post-war social contract defined by social democracy and the growing middle classes, but also underlying assumptions of superior cultural relationships retained from imperial times. Behind *Jugo*(-slavs) who were not always understood in a positive light there was a changing demographics, with fewer Slovenes and Croats and an increasing number of Serbs, Bosnians, and Macedonians, most of them unqualified manual laborers.

Neither Austria nor Yugoslavia had a policy on the permanent settlement of migrants in the receiving society. Both parties operated on the premise that the workers would return to their respective sending communities after their employment. In the case of Austria, this was understood as being when they were no longer needed, and in the case of Yugoslavia, after their working life ended. For Yugoslav negotiators, the class position was hard to articulate, but it emerged as a series of demands for guaranteed labor rights and protection. The unarticulated postcolonial relationship with the former imperial center was manifested in constant tensions concerning anti-social behavior on the part of workers, about which there were fears but which remained largely unaddressed. For the Austrian state, the issues surrounding the labor migrants revolved around responding to Yugoslav requests and minor practical issues. The country's policy was settled between the main party positions: the conservative ÖVP asserted that the workers should do their job and leave, whereas the SPÖ advocated more support for workers' social life and families, but neither party dealt with the issues of their class, marginalization, or inclusion.

Shaken by the nationalistic backlash of the early 1970s (the terrorist attacks and the nationalist outbreaks in Carinthia), the labor migrants' issues were eclipsed by questions of security and minority rights. These were two competing questions, the national minorities receiving more attention. As the structure of migration continued to evolve, no republics lobbied for migrants' interests, while Slovenia and Croatia actively advocated for the two respective minorities in Austria. The ethnic tensions and changing dynamics from within the group meant that the question of the *gastarbajteri* ceased to be of relevance in negotiations.

Abstracts

Diplomacy in Southeastern Europe. Interactions during Détente

Boštjan Udovič
"Going International": the (Non-)Importance of Non-Aligned Countries' Markets in the Foreign Economic Relations of Yugoslavia

This article examines the political and economic relations between Yugoslavia and countries of the Non-Aligned Movement (NAM). The analysis, conducted with different research methods, provides the following findings: (1) in Yugoslavia–NAM relations, politics was more important than economic benefits; (2) Yugoslav enterprises (known as Basic Organizations of Associated Labor) were in practice oriented more towards Western/capitalist markets and were less interested in NAM markets; (3) for ideological reasons (Yugoslavia's presumed hegemony in the NAM) and due to Yugoslav enterprises' low interest in operating in NAM markets, the Yugoslav authorities used different administrative measures to enhance economic cooperation with NAM countries, but with little success. The study thus concludes that the different expectations of both parties meant the economic cooperation between Yugoslavia and NAM countries was destined to fail from its very formation.
Keywords: Yugoslavia, foreign economic relations, Non-Aligned Movement, export, politics, economics

Tvrtko Jakovina
"Non-Alignment is not for Socialism". Yugoslav Non-Alignment during Détente

The period of détente was in many ways a fulfillment of most of Yugoslavia's foreign policy goals. Yugoslav–American relations were at an all-time high, with continuous exchange of top-level visits. In the second half of the 1970s, Yu-

goslavia managed to normalize its relations with the People's Republic of China. The role Belgrade played in Europe – especially within the Helsinki process, which led to the Final Declaration in 1975 – -was visible, constructive and considered beneficent. Yugoslavia was among the most active in the Group of Neutral and Non-aligned Countries, which institutionalized non-alignment policy in European political life. The Helsinki process helped Yugoslavia to finally receive diplomatic recognition of the Yugoslav–Italian border and speed up solving the minority question in Austria. The most problematic and dangerous aspects, especially for the internal stability of Yugoslavia, were relations with the Soviet Union. Non-alignment was the *leitmotiv* of all Yugoslav political goals and strategies; it was a foreign policy doctrine as well as a constitutive element of the ideology of Tito's Yugoslavia.
Keywords: Yugoslavia, Josip Broz Tito, foreign policy, Cold War, détente

Effie G. H. Pedaliu
The United States, Differentiation, and Balkan Cooperation during the Cold War

The policy of differentiation as an integral aspect of the policy of containment towards Communist Eastern Europe remains underexplored and its application and impact on the Balkan peninsula are still at an embryonic stage. The only country that has attracted systematic attention to date has been Romania. This essay considers the role of the Balkans in U.S. Cold War policy and examines the origins, evolution and implementation of the policy of differentiation in the region by successive U.S. presidents. It maps out how it affected the states of the peninsula across the Cold War divide. In parallel, it surveys how the policies and interests of the divided Balkan microcosm revealed the contradictions encapsulated in differentiation. It also depicts how the policy enabled consecutive bouts of regional cooperation across the Cold War divide and evaluates its efficacy against an evolving Cold War background.
Keywords: U.S. foreign policy, policy of differentiation, Cold War, détente, Balkan cooperation

Mišo Kapetanović
Yugoslav Labor Migrants Emerging as the Austrian Working Class (1960–1980)

What role did class and related cultural capital play in Austrian–Yugoslav bilateral relations? In the post-war Austria, the problem of class segregation was refractured by the ideology of social consolidation introduced with the post-Marshall plan prosperity. The image of weakening social class differences persisted in ignorance of incoming labor migration. As elsewhere in post-war Western Europe, the incoming migrants were allowed to work but sidelined in social integration and state protection, opening ground for the racialization of Yugoslavs, Turks, and other southern migrant groups as an underclass. The article explores how sociocultural difference was acknowledged, dealt with, and reproduced by the authors in the official documents of the Yugoslav state. The labor migrants were an important feature of the negotiations, but the article shows how class entanglements went beyond them and informed decisions of the state officials.

Keywords: class, bilateral agreements, Yugoslavia, Austria, détente

Reviews

Dieter J. Hecht/Eleonore Lappin-Eppel/Michaela Raggam-Blesch, Topographie der Shoah. Gedächtnisorte des zerstörten jüdischen Wien, Wien: Mandelbaum Verlag 2017, 3. überarb. Aufl., 605 Seiten.

Dieter J. Hecht/Michaela Raggam-Blesch/Heidemarie Uhl (Hg.), Letzte Orte vor der Deportation. Die Wiener Sammellager 1941/42, Wien/Berlin: Mandelbaum Verlag 2019, 261 Seiten.

„Topographie der Shoah", 2017 in der dritten überarbeiteten Auflage erschienen, ist ein Werk der Geschichtsschreibung, das die Vernichtung der Juden Wiens während der NS-Zeit ins Zentrum der Aufmerksamkeit stellt. Zugleich ist es ein Beitrag zur Erinnerungskultur, in dem die Gedächtnisorte des zerstörten jüdischen Wiens ausführlich beschrieben werden. Es bietet eine fundierte Grundlage für die weitere Vermittlung des Geschehens. Der Schwerpunkt der früheren Monographien und Sammelwerke zur Geschichte Wiens während der NS-Zeit seit etwa Mitte der 1970er-Jahre – der Standardwerke von Gerhard Botz und der Ergebnisse der Wiener Kommissionen zum „Anschluss 1938" –, lag mehr auf der Analyse der NS-Herrschaft und nahe am „Anschluss" im März/April 1938. Sie behandelten verschiedene Aspekte der NS-Herrschaft und beinhalteten einzelne wissenschaftliche Beiträge über den Holocaust.

Die von Hecht et al. verfasste Monographie deckt die Zeit von 1938 bis 1945 ab. Die Darstellung beginnt mit dem „Anschluss-Pogrom" in Wien, den Orten der Erniedrigung und Verfolgung, wie dem „Hotel Metropol", der Gestapo-Leitstelle Wien, die als der „zentrale Ort des Terrors" hervorgehoben wird; der Prozess der Arisierungen entlang der Ringstraße wird geschildert, dabei werden die NS-Behörden benannt und deren Adressen angegeben; der schrittweise berufliche Ausschluss, der Ausschluss jüdischer Kinder aus den Wiener Schulen, die Auflösung der Institutionen der Israelitischen Kultusgemeinde und die Funktionsweise der „Zentralstelle für jüdische Auswanderung" wie auch der Beginn von Flucht und Vertreibung konnten anhand markanter Orte der Stadt aufgezeigt werden; die Darstellung reicht von den Sammelwohnungen und -lagern, Zwischenstationen vor den Deportationen, aber auch den Zufluchtsorten in Wien, bis zu einer Auflistung der Zielorte der Deportationen aus Wien, der Konzentrations- und Vernichtungslager.

Die gewählten Gedächtnisorte sind Ausgangspunkte, von denen die AutorInnen Erinnerungen der Opfer wiedergeben. Bestimmte Orte, z. B. rund um die Wiener Urania, wurden aus Berichten, Briefen und Tagebüchern von Opfern, aber auch aus Aufzeichnungen der jüdischen Gemeinde, ausgewählt und zu „persönlichen Erinnerungsorten". Gedächtnisorte, dem Konzept Pierre Noras folgend, das in dem Buch allerdings nicht näher erläutert wird, können nicht nur räumlich sein. Sie können auch symbolisch sein, zudem als Orientierungspunkte dienen. Das Vermittlungskonzept bleibt etwas vage. Es handelt sich um keinen Stadtführer und kein Nachschlagewerk, aber es enthält Stadtpläne mit eingezeichneten Orten, die genauen Adressen sind jeweils angeführt und es ist zum Nachschlagen hilfreich. Ein Hinweis der AutorInnen, wie es didaktisch genutzt werden kann, fehlte bisher.

Anders ausgerichtet ist hingegen der Nachfolgeband „Letzte Orte. Die Wiener Sammellager und die Deportationen 1941/42". Dieses Buch wurde durch eine Ausstellung angeregt, die in Zusammenarbeit mit einem Team der Österreichischen Akademie der Wissenschaften entstanden ist und im Amtshaus Leopoldstadt in Wien gezeigt wurde. Von Interesse ist neuerlich der Wien-Bezug. Die letzten Orte vor der Deportation lagen für über 60.000 österreichische Opfer der Shoah vor allem der Jahre 1939 bis 1943 mitten in Wien. Sie waren in Sammellagern im Inneren der Stadt interniert, bevor sie, „wie es hieß", nach den Worten Rudolf Gelbards in der dem Ausstellungsband „Letzte Orte" (2019) vorausgegangenen Videodokumentation „Letzte Orte. Letzte Zeugen" (Regie: Frederick Baker, 2016), „nach dem Osten" deportiert wurden.

Der Ausstellungsband ergänzt das zuvor beschriebene Buch in hervorragender Weise. Die detaillierten Schilderungen anhand bisher nicht bearbeiteter amtlicher Quellen, Selbstzeugnisse und Fotos beleuchten von mehreren Seiten die Geschichte der Sammellager im 2. Bezirk – Kleine Sperlgasse, Castellezgasse und Malzgasse –, die von der „Zentralstelle für jüdische Auswanderung" zur Internierung in Wien eingerichtet wurden und aus denen die „Eichmann-Männer" die jüdischen Opfer durch die Stadt zum Aspangbahnhof (3. Bezirk) und zu anderen Bahnhöfen verfrachten ließen, von wo die Transporte in die Konzentrationslager weggingen.

Die Kapitel des Buches gliedern sich nicht mehr so sehr wie die zugrundeliegende Ausstellungskonzeption nach dem systematischen Vorgehen der NS-Stellen („Einberufen", Kennzeichnen, „Ausheben", im Lager, „Kommissionieren", Deportationen), sondern sind stärker an den Erinnerungen aus Interviews mit Zeitzeugen orientiert. Der Kapitelaufbau folgt der Einteilung in Opfer und Täter, wobei auch Porträts von IKG-Mitarbeitern, deren eindeutige Einordnung sich dieser Kategorien entzieht, vorkommen.

Die in der Folge in Berlin, Prag und Brünn nach dem Wiener Vorbild eingerichteten Zentralstellen, wie Monika Sommer und Heidemarie Uhl in der Einleitung des Buches hervorheben, dienten der Beschleunigung der Deportationen: „Die historische Bedeutung der Sammellager geht jedoch weit über Wien und Österreich hinaus. Sie repräsentieren die Rolle Wiens als Experimentierfeld für die Systematisierung und Radikalisierung der antijüdischen Maßnahmen des NS-Regimes und ab 1941 für die Organisation und Durchführung der Deportationen." Es ist mit Ausstellung und Buch beabsichtigt, diese weniger bekannten Orte der Stadt sichtbar werden zu lassen. Ausgehend von diesen lokalen Räumen versuchen die Beiträge des Ausstellungsbandes die größeren Dimensionen und quantitativen Ausmaße der Shoah anschaulich zu machen.

Jan Kreisky

Andrej Angrick, „Aktion 1005". Spurenbeseitigung von NS-Massenverbrechen 1942–1945, 2 Bde., Göttingen: Wallstein Verlag 2019, 2. Aufl., 1381 Seiten.

Bei der „Aktion 1005" handelte es sich um eines der geheimsten Projekte des „Dritten Reiches". Die eigenen Leute wurden per Schwur zu absolutem, lebenslangem Stillschweigen verpflichtet. Es ging um die restlose Beseitigung der Spuren der Massengräber im gesamten deutsch besetzten Europa: um das Ausgraben und Ausheben der Leichen, um das Verbrennen und zu Asche zermahlen und um die gärtnerische Tarnung des Areals. Dazu wurden Häftlingskommandos aus den Ghettos oder Lagern eingesetzt, die nach Abschluss der Aktion ermordet wurden. Dort, wo kein Opfer Zeugnis ablegen konnte, blieb die Vertuschungsaktion im Dunkeln, oftmals ist nicht einmal das 1005-Führungspersonal namentlich bekannt.

Nach einer kurzen Einleitung, in der Angrick sein methodisches Vorgehen darstellt, und einem Prolog, der sich u. a. mit den ersten Massenexekutionen im zweiten Halbjahr 1941 befasst, widmet er sich chronologisch dem Einsatz der „Aktion 1005" in den besetzten Gebieten der Sowjetunion bis zum Jahr 1944, und anschließend der Beseitigung der „kontaminierten Landschaften" im Generalgouvernement ab 1944. Ein besonderes Verdienst des Autors sind die beiden letzten Kapitel, die sich mit der Spurenverwischung am Balkan und mit jener in den Grenzen des „Reiches" beschäftigen – bislang ein Forschungsdesiderat.

Die bislang einzige umfassendere Studie zum Thema hat Jens Hoffmann vorgelegt,[1] der aber den Fokus auf die Sowjetunion und ausgewählte Orte im Generalgouvernement richtet. Ansonsten existieren nur regional- und lokalgeschichtliche Studien. Angrick versteht die Studie in Teilen als Quellenwerk, da die Herrschaftsquellen extrem dürftig sind. Verhörprotokolle und Aussagen von Opfern, Tätern und Zeugen müssen die kaum vorhandenen schriftlichen Quellen ersetzen. Er entschied sich zu einem narrativen Duktus, um den Tragödien der Opfer gerecht zu werden. Über Jahrzehnte hat er akribisch alle Ermittlungs- und Strafverfahren zum Gegenstand analysiert und in Dutzenden Archiven weltweit recherchiert. Allein der Anhang und das Register der fast 1400 Seiten umfassenden Studie betragen etwa 150 Seiten. Methodisch orientiert er sich an der

---

[1] Jens Hoffmann, „Das kann man nicht erzählen". ‚Aktion 1005' – Wie die Nazis die Spuren ihrer Massenmorde in Osteuropa beseitigten, Hamburg 2008.

Kriminalistik und der archäologischen Vorgangsweise, um nach dem Verfahren von Ausschluss und Plausibilität den empirischen Kern freizulegen. Angrick schreibt nicht exemplarisch. Das Buch ist voller Details und zeigt die gesamte Dimension des letzten Kapitels des Völkermordens. Selbst für den Rezensenten, der sich seit vielen Jahren dem Studium der Shoah widmet, ist das Lesen manchmal schier unerträglich.

Angrick beschränkt sich nicht auf die „Aktion 1005", sondern beschreibt auch ausführlich und detailliert die Massenvernichtung in den verschiedenen Vergasungsfabriken im Generalgouvernement und die zahllosen Massaker der Einsatzgruppen an sowjetischen Juden und Jüdinnen. Die ersten großen Judenmassaker mit jeweils weit mehr als 10.000 Opfern fanden ab Herbst 1941 statt. Sie blieben keineswegs geheim. Die lokale Bevölkerung war informiert, ebenso der Untergrund im Warschauer Ghetto oder die polnische Heimatarmee und der Vatikan. US-amerikanische, britische und sowjetische Medien berichteten etwa über das Massaker in der Kiewer Schlucht Babij Jar mit mehr als 30.000 Ermordeten und der Erschießung von 27.000 Jüdinnen und Juden im Wald von Rumbula bei Riga.

Erst ab der Jahreswende 1941/42, als die Offensive der deutschen Truppen im Osten scheiterte, begann Himmler mit Überlegungen, wie man die Spuren der Massenmorde auf sowjetischem Gebiet beseitigen könnte. Der Zeitpunkt war nicht zufällig, sondern fiel mit der „Wannseekonferenz" im Jänner 1942, wo die organisatorischen Grundlagen für die geplante Ermordung von zwölf Millionen Jüdinnen und Juden besprochen wurden, und mit dem Beginn der „Aktion Reinhardt", der Vernichtung aller im Generalgouvernement lebenden Jüdinnen und Juden ab März 1942, zusammen. Nachdem bereits 1941 Hunderttausende Jüdinnen und Juden in den eroberten Gebieten der Sowjetunion erschossen worden waren, begannen sich Heinrich Himmler und Reinhard Heydrich erst angesichts dieses monumentalen Vernichtungsprogramms die Frage zu stellen, wie man die Ermordeten nachhaltig beseitigen könnte. Die „Aktion 1005" war kein langfristiger Plan, der mit Beginn der Judenmassaker im Sommer 1941 bereits existierte, sondern war die Konsequenz der kumulativen Radikalisierung der Shoah.

Ende März 1942 wurde Paul Blobel, bislang Kommandeur des Sonderkommandos 4a, von Heydrich beauftragt, alle Massengräber im Osten ausfindig zu machen, die Leichen auszugraben, zu beseitigen und alle Spuren der Verbrechen zu verwischen. Mittlerweile wurden die verscharrten Leichen zu einem hygienischen Problem, da die ausströmenden Gase das Erdreich hoben und verweste Körper an die Oberfläche gelangten, das Grundwasser kontaminierten und akute Seuchengefahr bestand. Im Sommer 1942 begann die „Aktion 1005" mit der Aushebung der Massengräber in Chelmo/Kulmhof, wo die Opfer seit Dezember 1941 in einem Gaswagen erstickt worden waren. Nachdem der Einsatz von

Flammenwerfern, Sprengungen und diverse andere Versuche gescheitert waren, entschied man sich für einen Rost aus Metallschienen, worauf eine Schicht Leichen gestapelt wurde, darauf wurde eine Schicht Holzscheite gelegt und dann mit Benzin übergossen. Den Scheiterhaufen musste ein jüdischer Häftling besteigen und in Brand setzen, wobei dieser bei lebendigem Leib verbrannte. Dann wurden die Knochen mit einer Knochenmühle zermahlen. Nachdem die Spuren des Massenmords beseitigt waren, wurden die Häftlinge erschossen. Zwischen Sommer 1942 und Herbst 1943 wurden in den Vernichtungslagern Chelmo/Kulmhof, Auschwitz, Sobibor, Belzec, Treblinka und Majdanek auf diese Weise die Ermordeten zu Asche verbrannt. Ab dem Frühjahr 1943 verlagerte sich der Einsatz der „Aktion 1005" vorerst in die Ukraine und in den Süden der Sowjetunion. Dort konnte man nicht auf die in den Vernichtungslagern vorhandene Infrastruktur (Brennstoffe, Bagger usw.) zurückgreifen. Vorerst galt es, in diesem riesigen Raum die Lage der Massengräber zu erkunden. Dies gestaltete sich oftmals als schwierig, da keine zentralen Unterlagen existierten. Es entwickelte sich ein Rennen gegen die Zeit. Nach Stalingrad war die Rote Armee zügig nach Westen vorgedrungen und etwa in Rowno auf Massengräber gestoßen, die sie propagandistisch auswertete. Angrick macht deutlich, dass das Verwischen der Spuren letztlich scheiterte. Insbesondere in den bundesdeutschen Ermittlungs- und Strafverfahren kamen Hunderte Täter und überlebende Opfer zu Wort, die – aus unterschiedlicher Perspektive – das Grauenhafte schilderten.

Als kleine kritische Anmerkung sei erwähnt, dass sich Angrick bei den Vernichtungslagern Treblinka und Sobibor nicht auf die – seit einigen Jahren bekannten – Daten über die Anzahl der Gaskammern stützt, sondern den veralteten Aussagen Überlebender vertraut. Das ändert nichts daran, dass die Studie sicherlich das Standardwerk zum Thema ist, das in keiner einschlägigen Bibliothek und in keinem Buchregal von Shoahforscherinnen und Shoahforschern fehlen darf.

Walter Manoschek

Luciano Cheles/Alessandro Giacone (eds.), The Political Portrait. Leadership, Image and Power. From 1913 to the Present (Routledge Research in Art and Politics), New York: Routledge 2020, 368 Seiten.

Eine profunde Transformation der politischen Inszenierungskultur und der zunehmenden Alltäglichkeit von Porträts durch soziale Medien führen, so Luciano Cheles und Pierre Sorlin in der Einleitung zu ihrem Sammelband „The Political Portrait", zu einem Verlust von Teilen der Aura von Staatsoberhäuptern und Regierungschefs. Früher ernst und streng in marineblauen Anzügen, sind

Staatsoberhäupter und Regierungschefs heute wohlwollend und freundlich, lustig und gerne zu einem Selfie mit der Wählerschaft bereit. Tatsächlich erstaunt beim Betrachten der Bilder am Ende jedes Kapitels die Vielfalt der Porträtierten und der verwendeten Medien: von seriösen (und neuerdings lächelnden) Anzugträgern und Kostümträgerinnen, Karikaturen und Irritationen – wie die Bulldogge Churchill, der Pyjamaträger Dollfuß, der tanzende Jelzin und der Heiligen Obama – zu umjubelten, gestürzten und hängenden Diktatoren. Die Beiträge des Sammelbandes befassen sich entweder diachron mit den Staats- und Regierungschefs eines Landes (Italien, USA, Großbritannien, Russland, Deutschland, Frankreich, Nordkorea) oder dem Personenkult um einzelne autoritäre Herrscher (Österreich/Dollfuß, Spanien/Franco, China/Mao, Rumänien/Ceaușescu, Türkei/Atatürk und İnönü, Italien/Mussolini).[1] Aus dem Rahmen fällt der letzte Beitrag von Florian Göttke zu den brennenden US-Präsidenten-Bildnissen und Puppen im Irak, Iran und Afghanistan.

Was bei dieser Vielfalt fehlt, ist eine methodische, medienhistorische, kulturgeschichtliche und transnationale Klammer. So fragt man sich, ob sich Porträts wirklich nur dem politischen Regime und der Tradition im jeweiligen Land anpassen (S. 6), oder ob visuelle Einflüsse über politische und geographische Grenzen hinweg wirken.[2] Notwendig erscheinen außerdem eine klare Definition von visuellen Quellen und eine einheitliche methodische Herangehensweise an diese. Der knappe Verweis auf William J. T. Mitchell – „images as valuable documents in their own right" (S. XVIII) – im Vorwort genügt nicht. Gerade zum Thema des politischen Porträts bietet die Kunstgeschichte eine fundierte Basis, deren Fehlen hier eklatant ist. Es macht einen Unterschied, ob ein standardisiertes Porträt Mao Zedongs von über fünf Metern und einem Gewicht von 1,5 Tonnen auf dem Tian'anmen Platz in Peking hängt; ob die gemalten Porträts der Regierungschefs in der Galerie der Bundeskanzler in Berlin oder in der National Portrait Gallery in Washington hängen, entfernt oder umgehängt werden; ob das Porträt von Engelbert Dollfuß auf dem Klavier der Familie Schuschnigg zu finden ist; ob hinter İsmet İnönü und Celal Bayer ein Bild von Kemal Atatürk und hinter Angela Merkel ein Porträt Konrad Adenauers gemalt von Oskar Kokoschka (1966) hängt.

---

1 Die Zusammensetzung erklärt sich auch durch die Entstehung des Bandes aus einer Konferenz und Ausstellung im November 2013 in Paris zum Thema Porträts in der Propaganda in Italien und Frankreich in der Nachkriegszeit. Die Ergebnisse erschienen in einem Sammelband: Luciano Cheles/Alessandro Giacone (Hg.), Il ritratto e il potere. Immagini della politica in Francia e in Italia nel Novecento, Paris 2017.
2 Siehe den Vergleich von Hitler, Mussolini, Roosevelt und Stalin von Martin Loiperdinger/Rudolf Herz/Ulrich Pohlmann (Hg.), Führerbilder. Hitler, Mussolini, Roosevelt und Stalin in Fotografie und Film, München 1995.

Auch ist die Wahl der KünstlerInnen und AuftraggeberInnen keine zufällige. Oskar Kokoschka malte zum Beispiel Konrad Adenauer im Auftrag der Illustrierten „Quick". Wie Manja Wilkens in ihrem Beitrag zu den deutschen Kanzlern und der Kanzlerin zeigt, spielen Auftraggeber, Partei-Interessen und Geschmäcker ebenso eine Rolle wie die Abgrenzung vom nationalsozialistischen Kunstverständnis. Die Herausgeber hingegen sehen den Zweck von Porträts einzig darin, die PolitikerInnen in ihrem besten Licht abzubilden (S. 10–11). Den KünstlerInnen und FotografInnen wird eine eigene Bildsprache oder Motivation kaum zuerkannt. Die in den 1940er-Jahren aus dem Ausland in die Türkei zurückkehrenden KünstlerInnen hatten bestimmt mehr als nur Talent für die verherrlichende Darstellung İnönüs (S. 318) mitgebracht. Ebenso bildeten KünstlerInnen über die Jahrzehnte ihres Schaffens oft mehrere Persönlichkeiten ab. Als Beispiel kann die in den Beiträgen von Alessandro Giacone und Alessandra Antola Swan erwähnte Ghitta Carell genannt werden.[3] Die Fotografin mit jüdisch-ungarischen Wurzeln fotografierte neben Benito Mussolini, dessen Tochter Edda Ciano, die königliche Familie, Papst Pius XII und eben auch Italiens fünften Präsidenten, Guiseppe Saragat. Die Kontinuität ihres Schaffens über politische Zäsuren und ihre Verfolgung als Jüdin hinweg sowie der Entstehungs- und Verwendungszusammenhang der Porträts sind ebenso wichtig für die ikonographische Analyse der Bilder.

Eine große Neuerung sehen die Herausgeber im Auftauchen von Frauen in der politischen Bilderwelt. Spätestens hier vermisst man den Verweis auf die Monarchie. Die Bedeutung der parallel regierenden (oder exilierten) MonarchInnen sowie die lange historisch geformte und etablierte Bildsprache der HofmalerInnen und -fotografInnen wird unterschätzt. Zwei Beispiele: Die im Beitrag von Simon Downs analysierten Premierminister Großbritanniens regierten alle unter Queen Elizabeth. Visuelles Vorbild war sie nach Downs jedoch nur für die weibliche Premierministerin Margaret Thatcher (S. 70). Luciano Cheles beginnt seinen Beitrag mit einem Plakat der Familie des italienischen Monarchen Umberto II. Mit diesem wurde 1946 die Beibehaltung der Monarchie beworben. Der König setzte den zentralen Unterschied zu Demokratie und Diktatur visuell in den Fokus: die dynastische Nachfolgeregelung. Diese ist wichtig, denn sie erklärt die Versuche der Regierungschefs, eine solche Regelung visuell herzuleiten (siehe u. a. das erwähnte Dollfuß-Porträt auf dem Klavier der Schuschniggs).

Außerdem waren die Monarchien vorbildlich in der Distribution und Vermarktung von Porträts.[4] Im Sammelband finden sich in einigen Beiträgen

---

3 Eva Nodin, The Illusions of Ghitta Carell, in: Lena Johannesson/Gunilla Knape/Eva Dahlman (Hg.), Women photographers, European experience, Gothenburg 2004, 92–121; Roberto Dulio, Un ritratto mondano. Fotografie di Ghitta Carell, Monza 2013.
4 Siehe zur Monarchie insbesondere Alexis Schwarzenbach, Königliche Träume. Eine Kulturgeschichte der Monarchie von 1789 bis 1997, München 2012.

transnational agierende Akteure, Werbeagenturen, Spin-Doktoren und PR-Fachleute. So nennt Alessandra Antola Swan Quellen und Preislisten zum Vertrieb der zahlreichen Porträts Mussolinis. Die Stärke des Beitrages von Luciano Cheles liegt in der Erwähnung der Werbefirmen hinter den Kampagnen um die Präsidentschaft in Frankreich. Insbesondere die von Jacques Séguéla entwickelte „Force tranquille"-Kampagne um Françoise Mitterand wird zum Wendepunkt der Wahlkampfwerbung Frankreichs.

Eine Gemeinsamkeit der Beiträge ist der posthume Versuch der Abgrenzung zum Persönlichkeitskult der Diktatoren sowie das Verschwinden und Wiederauftauchen der Images. Zu Mao schreibt Stefan Landsberger: „China cannot do without the many faces of Mao" (S. 161). Dagegen schwankt der posthume Fall Nicolae Ceaușescu, geschildert von Manuela Marin, zwischen Ironie und Nostalgie, vom Vampir Ceaușescu bis zur misslungenen Büste in seinem Geburtsort. Auch der italienische „complesso del dittatore" war spätestens in den 1990er-Jahren nicht mehr ruhig zu stellen, wie Cheles in seinem Beitrag darlegt. Mehr mit dem Entstehen des Personenkults beschäftigen sich Christopher S. Wilson und Sinan Niyazioğlu in Bezug auf Kemal Atatürk und İsmet İnönü sowie der Beitrag von Franco Sorlin zu Francisco Franco. Ähnliche Mythen findet man auch in Nordkorea, wie Mary Ginsberg anhand von Beispielen aus Publikationen und ihr zugänglichen Ausstellungen verdeutlicht. Der Persönlichkeitskult um Kim Il Sung (Great Leader), Kim Jong Il (Dear Leader) und Kim Jong Un (Great Successor) sei der „most all-embracing ever known". Gerade das letzte Beispiel verdeutlicht eine Schwierigkeit in der Erforschung der Porträts von Staatsoberhäuptern: die Messbarkeit ihres Erfolgs und die tatsächliche emotionale Hingabe des Volkes (S. 182).

Der Sammelband fasst Vorhandenes zusammen und bleibt innerhalb der Grenzen der nationalen Geschichtsschreibung. Neuere Tendenzen, wie etwa die Kolonialgeschichte sowie außereuropäische Diktaturen aus einer nicht-westlichen Sicht zu inkludieren, werden nicht berücksichtigt.[5] Es obliegt den LeserInnen, das eigene Sehen zu hinterfragen und Vergleich zu ziehen.

Nathalie Patricia Soursos

---

5 Hierzu deutlich reflektierter der Sammelband Julia Adeney Thomas/Geoff Eley (eds.), Visualizing Fascism: The Twentieth-Century Rise of the Global Right, Durham 2020.

Authors

Tvrtko Jakovina, PhD.
Professor at the Department of History, University of Zagreb and guest lecturer in the MIREES Program, University of Bologna, tvrtko.jakovina@ffzg.hr

Mišo Kapetanović, PhD.
International Postdoctoral Fellow, School of Humanities and Social Science, University of St.Gallen, miso.kapetanovic@unisg.ch

Jan Kreisky, Mag.
Austrian Archives for Adult Education, Vienna, jan.kreisky@vhs.at

Walter Manoschek, ao. Univ.-Prof. Dr.
Department of Government, University of Vienna, walter.manoschek@univie.ac.at

Petra Mayrhofer, Dr.
Department of Contemporary History, University of Vienna, petra.mayrhofer@unive.ac.at

Effie G. H. Pedaliu, PhD.
Visiting Fellow at LSE IDEAS and a member of the UK Arts and Humanities Research Council Peer Review College, e.pedaliu@lse.ac.uk

Oliver Rathkolb, Univ.-Prof. DDr.
Head of the Department of Contemporary History, University of Vienna, oliver.rathkolb@univie.ac.at

Nathalie Patricia Soursos, Dr. MMag.
Institute of Byzantine and Modern Greek Studies, University of Vienna, nathalie.patricia.soursos@univie.ac.at

Boštjan Udovič, PhD.
Associate Professor, Centre of International Relations, University of Ljubljana,
bostjan.udovic@fdv.uni-lj.si

Zitierregeln

Bei der Einreichung von Manuskripten, über deren Veröffentlichung im Laufe eines doppelt anonymisierten Peer Review Verfahrens entschieden wird, sind unbedingt die Zitierregeln einzuhalten. Unverbindliche Zusendungen von Manuskripten als word-Datei an: agnes.meisinger@univie.ac.at

I. Allgemeines

Abgabe: elektronisch in Microsoft Word DOC oder DOCX.

Textlänge: 60.000 Zeichen (inklusive Leerzeichen und Fußnoten), Times New Roman, 12 Punkt, $1\frac{1}{2}$-zeilig. Zeichenzahl für Rezensionen 6.000–8.200 Zeichen (inklusive Leerzeichen).

Rechtschreibung: Grundsätzlich gilt die Verwendung der neuen Rechtschreibung mit Ausnahme von Zitaten.

II. Format und Gliederung

Kapitelüberschriften und – falls gewünscht – Unterkapiteltitel deutlich hervorheben mittels Nummerierung. Kapitel mit römischen Ziffern [I. Literatur], Unterkapitel mit arabischen Ziffern [1.1 Dissertationen] nummerieren, maximal bis in die dritte Ebene untergliedern [1.1.1 Philologische Dissertationen]. Keine Interpunktion am Ende der Gliederungstitel.

Keine Silbentrennung, linksbündig, Flattersatz, keine Leerzeilen zwischen Absätzen, keine Einrückungen; direkte Zitate, die länger als vier Zeilen sind, in einem eigenen Absatz (ohne Einrückung, mit Gänsefüßchen am Beginn und Ende).

Zahlen von null bis zwölf ausschreiben, ab 13 in Ziffern. Tausender mit Interpunktion: 1.000. Wenn runde Zahlen wie zwanzig, hundert oder dreitausend nicht in unmittelbarer Nähe zu anderen Zahlenangaben in einer Textpassage aufscheinen, können diese ausgeschrieben werden.

Daten ausschreiben: „1930er" oder „1960er-Jahre" statt „30er" oder „60er Jahre".

Datumsangaben: In den Fußnoten: 4.3.2011 [keine Leerzeichen nach den Punkten, auch nicht 04.03.2011 oder 4. März 2011]; im Text das Monat ausschreiben [4. März 2011].

Personennamen im Fließtext bei der Erstnennung immer mit Vor- und Nachnamen.

Namen von Organisationen im Fließtext: Wenn eindeutig erkennbar ist, dass eine Organisation, Vereinigung o. Ä. vorliegt, können die Anführungszeichen weggelassen werden: „Die Gründung des Oesterreichischen Alpenvereins erfolgte 1862." „Als Mitglied im

Womens Alpine Club war ihr die Teilnahme gestattet." **Namen von Zeitungen/Zeitschriften** etc. siehe unter „Anführungszeichen".

Anführungszeichen im Fall von Zitaten, Hervorhebungen und bei Erwähnung von Zeitungen/Zeitschriften, Werken und Veranstaltungstiteln im Fließtext immer doppelt: „"

Einfache Anführungszeichen nur im Fall eines Zitats im Zitat: „Er sagte zu mir: ‚….'"

Klammern: Gebrauchen Sie bitte generell runde Klammern, außer in Zitaten für Auslassungen: […] und Anmerkungen: [Anm. d. A.].

Formulieren Sie **bitte geschlechtsneutral bzw. geschlechtergerecht.** Verwenden Sie im ersteren Fall bei Substantiven das Binnen-I („ZeitzeugInnen"), nicht jedoch in Komposita („Bürgerversammlung" statt „BürgerInnenversammlung").

Darstellungen und Fotos als eigene Datei im jpg-Format (mind. 300 dpi) einsenden. Bilder werden schwarz-weiß abgedruckt; die Rechte an den abgedruckten Bildern sind vom Autor/von der Autorin einzuholen. Bildunterschriften bitte kenntlich machen: Abb.: Spanische Reiter auf der Ringstraße (Quelle: Bildarchiv, ÖNB).

Abkürzungen: Bitte Leerzeichen einfügen: vor % oder €/zum Beispiel z. B./unter anderem u. a.

Im Text sind möglichst wenige allgemeine Abkürzungen zu verwenden.

III. Zitation

Generell keine Zitation im Fließtext, auch keine Kurzverweise. Fußnoten immer mit einem Punkt abschließen.

Die nachfolgenden Hinweise beziehen sich auf das Erstzitat von Publikationen.
Bei weiteren Erwähnungen sind Kurzzitate zu verwenden.
- Wird hintereinander aus demselben Werk zitiert, bitte den Verweis **Ebd./ebd.** bzw. mit anderer Seitenangabe **Ebd., 12./ebd., 12.** gebrauchen (kein Ders./Dies.), analog: Vgl. ebd.; vgl. ebd., 12.
- Zwei Belege in einer Fußnote mit einem **Strichpunkt**; trennen: Gehmacher, Jugend, 311; Dreidemy, Kanzlerschaft, 29.
- Bei Übernahme von direkten Zitaten aus der Fachliteratur **Zit. n./zit. n.** verwenden.
- Indirekte Zitate werden durch **Vgl./vgl.** gekennzeichnet.

Monografien: Vorname und Nachname, Titel, Ort und Jahr, Seitenangabe [ohne „S."].

Beispiel Erstzitat: Johanna Gehmacher, Jugend ohne Zukunft. Hitler-Jugend und Bund Deutscher Mädel in Österreich vor 1938, Wien 1994, 311.

Beispiel Kurzzitat: Gehmacher, Jugend, 311.
Bei mehreren AutorInnen/HerausgeberInnen: Dachs/Gerlich/Müller (Hg.), Politiker, 14.

Reihentitel: Claudia Hoerschelmann, Exilland Schweiz. Lebensbedingungen und Schicksale österreichischer Flüchtlinge 1938 bis 1945 (Veröffentlichungen des Ludwig-

Boltzmann-Institutes für Geschichte und Gesellschaft 27), Innsbruck/Wien [bei mehreren Ortsangaben Schrägstrich ohne Leerzeichen] 1997, 45.

Dissertation: Thomas Angerer, Frankreich und die Österreichfrage. Historische Grundlagen und Leitlinien 1945–1955, phil. Diss., Universität Wien 1996, 18–21 [keine ff. und f. für Seitenangaben, von–bis mit Gedankenstich ohne Leerzeichen].

Diplomarbeit: Lucile Dreidemy, Die Kanzlerschaft Engelbert Dollfuß' 1932–1934, Dipl. Arb., Université de Strasbourg 2007, 29.

Ohne AutorIn, nur HerausgeberIn: Beiträge zur Geschichte und Vorgeschichte der Julirevolte, hg. im Selbstverlag des Bundeskommissariates für Heimatdienst, Wien 1934, 13.

Unveröffentlichtes Manuskript: Günter Bischof, Lost Momentum. The Militarization of the Cold War and the Demise of Austrian Treaty Negotiations, 1950–1952 (unveröffentlichtes Manuskript), 54–55. Kopie im Besitz des Verfassers.

Quellenbände: Foreign Relations of the United States, 1941, vol. II, hg. v. United States Department of States, Washington 1958.
[nach Erstzitation mit der gängigen Abkürzung: FRUS fortfahren].

Sammelwerke: Herbert Dachs/Peter Gerlich/Wolfgang C. Müller (Hg.), Die Politiker. Karrieren und Wirken bedeutender Repräsentanten der Zweiten Republik, Wien 1995.

Beitrag in Sammelwerken: Michael Gehler, Die österreichische Außenpolitik unter der Alleinregierung Josef Klaus 1966–1970, in: Robert Kriechbaumer/Franz Schausberger/Hubert Weinberger (Hg.), Die Transformation der österreichischen Gesellschaft und die Alleinregierung Klaus (Veröffentlichung der Dr.-Wilfried Haslauer-Bibliothek, Forschungsinstitut für politisch-historische Studien 1), Salzburg 1995, 251–271, 255–257.
[bei Beiträgen grundsätzlich immer die Gesamtseitenangabe zuerst, dann die spezifisch zitierten Seiten].

Beiträge in Zeitschriften: Florian Weiß, Die schwierige Balance. Österreich und die Anfänge der westeuropäischen Integration 1947–1957, in: Vierteljahrshefte für Zeitgeschichte 42 (1994) 1, 71–94.
[Zeitschrift Jahrgang/Bandangabe ohne Beistrichtrennung und die Angabe der Heftnummer oder der Folge hinter die Klammer ohne Komma].

Presseartikel: Titel des Artikels, Zeitung, Datum, Seite.
Der Ständestaat in Diskussion, Wiener Zeitung, 5. 9. 1946, 2.

Archivalien: Bericht der Österr. Delegation bei der Hohen Behörde der EGKS, Zl. 2/pol/57, Fritz Kolb an Leopold Figl, 19. 2. 1957. Österreichisches Staatsarchiv (ÖStA), Archiv der Republik (AdR), Bundeskanzleramt (BKA)/AA, II-pol, International 2 c, Zl. 217.301-pol/57 (GZl. 215.155-pol/57); Major General Coleman an Kirkpatrick, 27. 6. 1953. The National Archives (TNA), Public Record Office (PRO), Foreign Office (FO) 371/103845, CS 1016/205
[prinzipiell zuerst das Dokument mit möglichst genauer Bezeichnung, dann das Archiv, mit Unterarchiven, -verzeichnissen und Beständen; bei weiterer Nennung der Archive bzw. Unterarchive können die Abkürzungen verwendet werden].

Internetquellen: Autor so vorhanden, Titel des Beitrags, Institution, URL: (abgerufen Datum). Bitte mit rechter Maustaste den Hyperlink entfernen, so dass der Link nicht mehr blau unterstrichen ist.
Yehuda Bauer, How vast was the crime, Yad Vashem, URL: http://www1.yadvashem.org/yv/en/holocaust/about/index.asp (abgerufen 28.2.2011).

Film: Vorname und Nachname des Regisseurs, Vollständiger Titel, Format [z.B. 8 mm, VHS, DVD], Spieldauer [Film ohne Extras in Minuten], Produktionsort/-land Jahr, Zeit [Minutenangabe der zitierten Passage].
Luis Buñuel, Belle de jour, DVD, 96 min., Barcelona 2001, 26:00–26:10 min.

Interview: InterviewpartnerIn, IntervieweriIn, Datum des Interviews, Provenienz der Aufzeichnung.
Interview mit Paul Broda, geführt von Maria Wirth, 26.10.2014, Aufnahme bei der Autorin.

Die englischsprachigen Zitierregeln sind online verfügbar unter: https://www.verein-zeitgeschichte.univie.ac.at/fileadmin/user_upload/p_verein_zeitgeschichte/zg_Zitierregeln_engl_2018.pdf

Es können nur jene eingesandten Aufsätze Berücksichtigung finden, die sich an die Zitierregeln halten!